SOCIAL MAGNETISM

How to have fun building meaningful relationships with brilliant business minds

Ben Chai
With Nate Chai

STORY WAND

YOU WAVE IT. WE MAKE IT.

Published by StoryWand, London

Helping busy entrepreneurs quickly produce and share their high-impact message and story. StoryWand. You Wave it, we make it.

www.StoryWand.co

Visit the author's Facebook page at

https://www.facebook.com/BenInsightChai/

Cover Vectors Created by Freepik

Interior Typesetting by Derek Murphy

ISBN-13: 978-1546489030

ISBN-10: 1546489037

10 9 8 7 6 5 4 3 2 1

CONTENTS

Introduction

W h y   w e   w r o t e   t h i s b o o k

IT WAS AROUND THE 10TH NETWORKING event of my life that I felt that something was... amiss. It was close to the 50th that I started to get a handle on what was wrong with the events I was going to. Finally, after attending hundreds of events was I finally able to vocalise what my issue was.

I hated networking.

I hated the constant sales pitches, I hated the faux

1

niceties, but most of all I hated how much of my time it was taking. I was going to three networking events a week, spending 12 hours Monday to Friday (and the occasional weekend tradeshow) standing around in a suit meeting people who, although excellent business people, I wasn't gelling with.

And then, suddenly! A breakthrough!

After another night of meeting new people, my inner pocket brimming with business cards to follow-up on the next day, I realised what I was doing wrong. I love meeting people, I love spending time with passionate people, I love connecting people and seeing those relationships come to fruition, so *why was I having such a bad time?*

Night after night I met people that wore suits of armour with Italian labels. I met people so well trained at meeting people that I felt like I was a hand-shaking conveyor belt. Everyone was so polite, so formal, so... unbalanced. Not "unbalanced" in an insane way, I mean in a way that was too shiny, too pristine. I was looking for business partners, and I needed to see if after they'd been through the mud and muck, they'd still have that smile, composure, and grace.

Whether a vendor, supplier, or client, if you buy from or sell to someone, you are in *business* with them. To be in business with someone, you've got to know that they're a good bet and see how committed to you they are when under pressure.

This book was created to detail the daily strategies and techniques to help you find, talk to, and magnetically attract the right people into your life. Using these techniques will make it possible for you to not meet amazing, genuine, go-getting people. Half the time, these people will be ones that approach you!

HOW TO TELL IF YOU'RE READY FOR THIS BOOK

If, like me, you're looking to draw incredibly smart business minds into your circle then you're in the right place. But before we delve into the details, I'd like to make a confession. Not everyone is ready to receive and act on the information shared. Not everyone is ready because it takes them out of their comfort zone.

As you work through this book, you will need the strength to push yourself outside your comfort zone. This will help you develop a confidence that enables you to be authentic in every situation A magnetic authenticity that doesn't come naturally and is a skill that this book will help you develop.

The second must-have is the time and drive to sit-down and complete the written exercises. I've personally read hundreds of books like this. The *only* books that helped me were the books whose lessons I actively put into my life. A book is worthless if you mentally accept the content without taking the specific actions outlined in the book's lessons.

Finally, you will need to have a desire to create something bigger than yourself. This desire may be a business, a charitable project, or even change the zeitgeist of our age! It doesn't matter what stage of the journey you're at, if you've just had an idea, are a solo-preneur treading water, or if you've got 100,000 followers on Twitter. You need to have something that's greater than *you*. Why?

Greatness attracts greatness.

Unless you're working toward something phenomenal you won't find phenomenal people that want to be a part of what you're doing.

What you're going to get from reading this book

This book will help you evolve your inner and outer worlds, to ensure that the two worlds are congruent with each other. Congruency is when your outer world reflects your inner beliefs and understanding about the types of people you *should* be hanging out with.

As you complete the book's exercises, your inner world will evolve and you will:

- Gain a deep understanding of the value you can provide to others

- Build an authentic confidence that will radiate out of yourself

- Build an innate charm of compassion, and

empathy that will help you figure out what people *really* want

- At the same time, your outer world will evolve and help you:

- Build a life around like-minded people who will help you reach higher levels in the areas you wish to develop and improve

- Clearly understand what high-performance, high-achieving people value, and how to provide that value

- Create a personal narrative around your life that changes people's perspective from, "Who is this person?" to "Who *IS* this person?!"

The next ten chapters take you on a journey that will help you develop become socially magnetic in your business and personal life. Social magnetism will help integrate your business life you're your personal life so that they don't feel so...at odds. Finally, the skills will help you deepen your relationships with friends and family, by developing a wider understanding of communication.

Every exercise and lesson has been developed to help you avoid the mistakes I made in a variety of situations. Thank you for working with this book. It was an absolute blast to write and I am excited to share these lessons that will help you become Socially Magnetic.

Nate Chai

Nate@Chai.co.uk

17/7/2017

A Note from the "Dr. Who of Business"

WHATEVER YOUR STATUS AND PERSONAL AMBITIONS, one important life skill is the ability to connect and socialise effectively. The ability to connect effectively opens doors of infinite possibility to you.

We all have written or unwritten goals in our lives. Here are several scenarios where it becomes painfully obvious how important the ability to connect is:

- You require funding, partnerships, or more sales.

- You have been made redundant and desperately need a new job.

- You want to find a life partner who loves you for you.

- You are in urgent need of the right medical expertise.

- You want to have a long-lived career.

- You want to get a promotion.

- You work in the servicing industry and want to get more tips.

You can quickly see from the above scenarios that the adage, *"it isn't what you know, it's who you know,"* is still relevant in today's world of social media, and screen-to-screen interactions.

The ability to effectively connect with and socialise will enable you to reach any goal you have today or in the future.

This book contains many great tricks and tips to help you effectively network at events. These events could be a friend's party, a dinner, an exhibition, a seminar, a political or religious gathering, online in a forum or whichever social media outlets (Facebook, Twitter, LinkedIn, Instagram and so on) you enjoy participating in.

Every technique shared will help you in every area whether it be business, life partners, or finding the right connections.

You will also benefit from the exercises contained

at the end of each chapter. As you work through these exercises, you will gradually become one of the most effective networking and sociability experts in your area.

Remember, for many a network event is scary. Focus on how you can become an Oasis in the Storm of this scariness. Connect rather than just network.

Finally, do send us stories of your successes.

Ben Chai

Ben@Lanix.co.uk

19/7/2017

BEN CHAI

CHAPTER 1:
Social Magnetism 101

11

Understand the playing field

THE MAJORITY OF PEOPLE ARE *TERRIBLE* at sharing with people. Talk at, talk to but never share with. However, it gets worse. Have you ever tried to say "hello" to a stranger in the street, coffee shop, or on public transport in a busy city or a highly developed country? Most often, their first thought is, *"what does this person want?"* Some immediately class you in the same realm as pickpockets, beggars, and people trying to get you to sign up for a charity.

One of the *most - if not the most* - important skill set for an entrepreneur is the ability to network effectively. Wouldn't it be great if you could say "hello" to anyone and get a good response?! Wouldn't it be fantastic if instead of you having to open up a conversation, people would magically come up to you and want to share with you in the street?

This book is about how to develop social magnetism. Social magnetism is the ability to attract people so that they naturally want to come and talk with you. This ability doesn't come overnight, so to help, this book will help you design and build your own unique conversational framework and sprinkle it with the magic ingredient that will literally help you become a people magnet.

Be prepared to put yourself in situations outside your comfort zone. As you develop your social magnetism framework, you will need to test your conversational skills in environments where (ironically) it is tough to find people that know how to actually connect, the networking event!

EVENT NETWORKING

Networking events are excellent places to build your skillset and to practice the basics of social magnetism. Although people may be unskilled at how to network, they would love to meet and connect with people. The key word in that last sentence is *connect.* In today's world of branding, marketing and drop in/drop out social media conversations, the ability to authentically connect has long been forgotten.

A networking event is a good secure place to learn to effectively connect. Once you learn the skills of value-add, being relevant and are able to make people feel special, you will become socially magnetic. At this point people will want you to share about your business, project or requests for support. A network event will also give you the opportunity to study people that are already socially magnetic, *and* understand why other people *aren't*.

Let's get started with the basics. To succeed at an event, you will need to learn how to prepare for an event, locate people you can help, get their details and finally connect afterwards.

Sounds simple enough, right? Let me [Nate] share several lessons from my past.

For some bizarre reason, most people *hate* networking. They hate the term "networking", they hate the very thought of going to a "networking event", they hate networking so much that they scoff when you tell them that you're going "networking".

I remember one time when I was having a conversation with a colleague and they asked me what

I was doing that evening. I told them I was going to a networking event; their eyes became moist, they grabbed both of my hands, and whispered: "The world's not a fair place."

To be fair to my colleague, the worst networking experience I ever had was akin to my Year-5 school disco. I stood in the corner, dressed in my nice clothes, clutching my beverage, and watched people effortlessly converse and share their thoughts and ideas.

After that fateful evening (the networking event, *not* my Year 5 disco), I swore that I would become the greatest networker that has ever lived! Well, maybe not the *greatest* but I made a promise to myself never to waste that amount of time again. Now, after countless hours spent chatting to people from all kinds of industries, here are the five biggest mistakes I made when I started networking.

TAKING BEFORE GIVING

When I began to attend networking events, I would try to absorb all the knowledge I could – I was a ruthless information hound. When I entered a conversation, I would drop the bomb "What do you do?" followed by "Tell me everything I need to know." I fell into the isolation trap. The isolation trap is self-created by a personality that no-one wants to engage with. The constant bombardment of others with questions is one such personality.

In fact, this was the reason why my colleague *hated* networking so much: they saw it as a den of jackals all foaming at the mouth to get information. But that's not the case at all.

Now that I'm more experienced I know how this feels from the other side. When you *only* seek information, and when you *only* look to see what *you* can get out of a conversation, it makes the people around you feel used and inhuman. When Ben meets people like this, you will literally see him excuse himself and never return to speak with that person again.

The constant question bombardment will make it unlikely that people will want to connect with you but will also avoid you whenever they see you at other events.

To avoid the isolation trap (and feel better about yourself in the process) you need to create a value blueprint. The value blueprint contains all the areas you can help someone with or connect with them over. Use the power of ten. Sit down and write a list of:

- ten skills that you have

- ten great people you know (and what they do)

- ten subjects you have a lot of experience with. Note the key word *experience* as opposed to theoretical knowledge.

This is your value blueprint. You now know what skills you have that can help people, the high-value people who you can connect others to, and know the list of topics that you can share experienced advice about.

Once you realise the areas where you can help others, you can use this unbelievably powerful line (when it's appropriate): "Perhaps I can help you with that, would you mind if I share a little?"

This question is powerful because it shows you have been listening to the conversation and that instead of rudely hi-jacking the conversation you've asked their permission to share. It is better to "share" rather than "talk at" as we never know people's full set of experiences until we get to know them better.

You will experience three responses. "No" (unlikely), "not right now" or "yes". The responses are all irrelevant because each response provides you with an opportunity to shine. "No" and "Not right now" provides you with an opportunity to send them a concerned letter and insights at a later stage.

When you show you've remembered a conversation and followed it up, people are far more likely to remember you, want to know more about you and will include you in future conversations.

For those that say "yes," you now have an opportunity to share some experience that may be valuable to your new contact. It may even result in you offering to do a favour for your new contact. Doing a favour for someone is a great way to add value to someone and create a further connection. This action alone is a great way to advertise your personal brand. If it helps the other person and you are at a business event, they may even be willing to give you a testimonial for your service.

However, don't expect much in return for your favour; imagine yourself as a supermarket worker handing out free samples to shoppers. The supermarket is not trying to sell that product there and then, they're generating interest in the product. Similarly, unless you know people well, your goal *isn't* to close a sale at a networking event: it's to get someone *interested* in the possibility of doing business with you.

DO:

- Think about *all* the value you can provide

- Make sure *you* like the other person. There's no point in starting a dialogue with someone who you don't think you can do business with

- Leverage your own network. Although you may not be able to help someone, you may know someone who can. When you help others with no financial gain in return, people will appreciate and want to return the favour.

DON'T:

- Give away your product for free (unless you get something you want in return). You're offering a taster of your services, or of your personality, or of your network.

- Undervalue your product or yourself – giving away value for free does not mean that you or your product is now worthless

Talking too much

AFTER I MADE MY LIST I BEGAN TO REALISE how I could add value to other people; the problem was I wouldn't shut up about it. As soon as I heard a conversational opportunity... I pounced! Sharing all the wonderful things I could do, how I'd do them, and how it would benefit the listener.

The mistake I'd made is that other people were also there to show off what they could do for others. By hogging the limelight, I prevented others from having a great experience and stifled any opportunities for myself. This was due to two reasons.

The first was that, instead of coming off as helpful and intriguing, I came off as needy and cloying. It was clear to the people around me that I was simply looking for people to "owe" me a favour. Through trying to provide this huge amount of value, people felt like I was trying to subjugate them by putting them into my debt.

I was too desperate to prove that I could help others, and told them everything I could do. I didn't tailor what I was saying to the listener. Essentially, I was rattling off my skill list in the hope that one of those skills would hit my listener's requirements. It made me seem desperate and like I was overcompensating for a potential lack of value.

The second was that *other people want to show off too.* I thought I could help everybody, so as soon as a problem was mentioned *I* would instantly offer my help. This meant that others didn't feel like they could shine, or start relationships.

I was still being selfish. I had gone too far the opposite way of being an information hoarder. I was a favour hoarder, constantly trying to one-up the people around me, and show that I was the most valuable person in the room.

By talking too much and offering too much value I intimidated the people around me, and made myself look desperate and needy. On a related note, I ended up helping people who I didn't particularly like, and who I didn't really want to help. If I had listened more, I could've avoided all that and found who it was that I'd like to work with and exactly *how* I could help them.

DO:

- Listen more. Get a detailed understanding of someone *before* offering any actual help

- Hold back. Like a date, you don't want someone overloading you with *all* their amazing qualities; it's far more impressive if you let them discover your qualities over time.

DON'T:

- Dominate conversations. Everyone there is trying to present themselves in their best light; if you're talking all the time, others won't have an opportunity.

- Immediately offer a solution. After someone mentions an issue or problem, ask them a question about it.

Later on, approach them and ask them about the problem again, and (if you like them) say something like, "I was *thinking* about the challenge you shared with us and I believe I may have a few solutions that can help resolve that challenge." If they are interested in speaking with you further, then arrange a phone call or meeting.

The key word in the sentence is "thinking." The reason is that the event attendee will understand that you weren't just interested in selling them any solution. Instead, you had spent some time considering (thinking) about what the event attendee had said and had thought of solutions which may help the attendee.

Talking too little

AFTER GETTING NOWHERE SCREAMING ABOUT MY VALUE and making people thoroughly uncomfortable, I evolved my style into one of a cool, collect, quiet business genius. Silent, and cunning, rarely speaking... but that too proved to be less than useful.

You need to be able to show yourself off, you need to demonstrate that you are a valuable person to know, and you can't do that if you don't say anything.

People love to talk about themselves; it's a strange quirk of psychology that the more we tell someone about ourselves the closer we feel to them. So, it's important to allow others in the conversation to express themselves... to a point.

The actual leap from sharing too much to sharing too little is huge, one that takes a lot of practice to master. However, one good way to ensure that you talk just the right amount is to steer the conversation.

In a group situation introduce everyone and use open questions and body language to develop a group conversation. For example, if one attendee is doing the majority of the talking, step in and look at another person in the group and say, "That was a great point, what's your perspective on what we're discussing?"

NB: The phrase "what we're discussing" is used as a general comment. In a live conversation it is best to be specific. If the conversation was about fear and failure, ask another person, what their perspective on fear and failure is.

By including everyone in the conversation, and giving people an opportunity to speak, people will understand that you're trying to help as many people as you can. Oddly enough, if you don't offer an opinion on something, you'll get asked what you think about it, and *then* you should offer what value you can provide.

DO:

- Imagine yourself as the director of the conversation. Encourage quieter members to speak up and share opinions.

- Ask questions you feel others may want to know answers to. If someone is talking about something you don't understand then ask for further explanation. Nine times out of ten, a conversation participant has later thanked me for asking the question.

- Leave conversations in which someone is talking *way* too much. Asking for other people's opinions in that environment will result in a power struggle between yourself and the speaker – it's best avoided, so leave.

DON'T:

- Deflect attention away from you. When asked a question you need to answer it impeccably, and in a way that invites more discussion (more about this later).

- Be afraid to interject at points. Interruptions are always rude, but when you ask for further explanation (e.g. "Can you help me understand what you meant by your last point?"), it is often helpful to both the speaker and those around you.

No follow up

B Y THIS POINT I HAD EMERGED FROM MY AWKWARD cocoon and become a social butterfly, except no one was sending me emails! I must've given out 100 business cards, and not a single email had fluttered back my way.

For days afterwards, I was still pondering this mystery. Until I opened one of my desk drawers at work... and found a massive cache of business cards! Then it dawned on me: most people *do the exact same thing as me* – they take the business card, throw it in a drawer, and forget all about it.

But you can be different! A simple email will do, or a call, or a LinkedIn message. Anything that says, "It actually *was* great meeting you and I didn't just take your business card out of politeness."

Networking is about connecting and building relationships, networking events is the catalyst for you to start them.

Once you have someone's details, go the extra mile. Add dates in your calendar that automatically remind you to send a message to someone to see how they're doing.

DO:

- Write some interesting facts about the person on their business card. This will help remind you what they do and help build rapport with them.

- Sent some form of contact ASAP. For example, send an email, add them on LinkedIn, and give them a call the next day

- Invest time or money into building a Rolodex (a spreadsheet will do) with basic information, and a schedule of when you to contact them.

DON'T:

- Feel the need to contact *everybody*. Quality is much more important than quantity. As you improve your networking ability, you will eventually have so many good contacts that you won't have the time to contact everyone.

- Wait for a business card. If you think you'd like to do business with them, add them on LinkedIn or Facebook there and then.

Network infrequently

FINALLY, I THOUGHT I WAS AN EXPERT AT NETWORKING. So I stopped. I quit. I thought I didn't need it anymore.

Big mistake.

I slipped, my edges dulled. No longer was I on the ball. Things would happen that I'd find out about *weeks* after the event had taken place. Other people would get these amazing opportunities that I'd miss out on. I started to see meeting people as a chore again.

By regularly going to business events you expose yourself to a lot of opportunity. Everyone is there to meet *someone*. People go to business events *because* they want to find people who they can do business with.

Similarly, the amount of knowledge you gain from attending a business event catapults your success. It's not just industry knowledge, it's about learning communication skills, it's about understanding how different people do business, and it's about seeing what works and what doesn't.

What I have since done is create a regular networking schedule. You can find business events for almost every day of the week. However, I would warn against networking every night of the week, as it will negatively impact on your non-business relationships.

Today, I attend one or two networking events a week to hone and refine my social magnetism, and keep my knowledge current. It's amazing how much you learn from a conversation with someone who has a different perspective from you.

DO:

- Give yourself a couple of evenings a week to go to network event.

- Vary the networking events that you go to. Having knowledge about multiple industries will open up far more doors for you than sticking to just one industry. Remember a networking event does not just have to be business oriented. For example, Ben networks with several hundred people from all walks of life when he goes salsa dancing

DON'T:

- Skip an event. The keys here are *consistency* and meeting new people part of your routine. Ben has made several good friends and business partners by turning up to a weekly salsa event. These friends and business associates would not have been made if he turned up to one or two and then quit.

- Go without a purpose. In the beginning, your goal might be to "talk to five people"; as you get better that will evolve into "find seven people I can give value to". You *need* a goal for the evening

- Stop pushing yourself. Complacency is a killer. Find new ways to improve and do new things at networking events. For example, if you find people's eyes are glazing over or they walk away at certain points in the conversation, work out why and what you can do to end each conversation on a high point.

PRE-PREPARATION

So far you've learned several good conversational tips. However, these tips will be sabotaged if you have not prepared in advance for the event. For example, if you have not eaten beforehand you may feel and act a bit grumpy towards others.

We won't go into detail but here are several essential things you must do in advance to make things smoother for you at an event.

- Brush teeth

- Wash

- Bring business cards

- Ensure phone is fully charged

- Bring pen and notepad/ laptop

- Bring a great attitude

- Bring food and drink

- Bring money for entrance fee, travel, and drinks if you are not bringing your own bottle of water

Chapter 1: Key take-aways

I HATE THE TERM "NETWORKING" because it makes what you're actually doing seem cold, and calculated. What you're really doing at these events is socializing and connecting (albeit with a business focus). The most valuable aspect of encouraging yourself to improve your networking capability is because this skill is easily transferable to other areas of your life.

For example, if you go to a party, you can use the skills developed from attending all the networking events. These skills will help you meet people who like you and appreciate your company. The conversation topics are (of course) different, but the intended outcome is the same.

If you are single, the same principles are also effective for finding a partner. These skills are useful even at family gatherings! Christmas, birthdays, and New Year's Eve. It's *all* communication. The principles again are:

- **Give something:** Give knowledge, add value, help people, and you'll be surprised at how much easier everything gets.

- **Listen more:** Other people want to talk and if you're yapping a lot you appear selfish and not genuine.

- **Don't talk too little:** Use the conversation to find out what you'd like to know about the others involved; if you're attentive and interested someone *will* ask for your opinion.

- **Follow up:** A quick call or email goes much further than people think it does.

- **Keep it regular:** Incorporate networking into your lifestyle, you needn't overdo it.

Chapter 1 Exercises

EXERCISE 1 - WRITE DOWN YOUR VALUE

WRITE DOWN 10 SUBJECTS YOU KNOW ABOUT and can offer help with or a perspective on in any conversation. Write down a brief explanation of why you have the knowledge and experience in that area.

NB: Your experience and personal stories offer far more value than knowledge without the experience.

As an example, here are ten of mine.

Eczema: Having suffered from eczema all my life I have a lot of knowledge about what works and what hinders and makes eczema worse.

Salsa dancing: Having danced salsa for over twenty years, I know the best UK clubs, the best congresses to attend and the strengths and weaknesses of many of the international salsa teachers and I also know over a hundred moves and body movements.

Writing: I've been a professional writer and editor for over two decades. I've written internal newsletters, corporate blogs, editorial content, books, marketing material so I have a lot of knowledge about what works and what doesn't work in any given situation and scenario for any specific audience.

Parenting: I have two grown up children. I have parented them though their toddler stage, to their child stage, to their teenage stage, to their pre-adult stage. Each stage is different and required different parenting techniques to help them move to the next stage.

Super-heroes and comics: I love superheroes and comic books and used to collect them as a child. If anyone is interested on the strengths and weaknesses of any hero and how true to comic the film and TV portrayals of these characters are, I'm there.

Mathematics: My degree is in mathematics – mathematics enabled to see many aspects of life and business in terms of patterns. I can also help people and their children in improving their financial and numeracy skills.

Social media marketing: Being a writer and editor, I have had decades of writing content for well-known brands such as Microsoft, British Telecom, Citi bank and then promoting the content using Facebook, Twitter, LinkedIn, YouTube and Instagram.

Working in the service industry: In my younger days, I worked in a pub and a hostel so I have a lot of stories and experience from working in this industry.

Property investment: I have invested in property for three decades and weathered several property crashes. As a result, I can share about successful property investment strategies, recovering and weathering a property crash and dealing with the many people essential to the property eco-system.

Travel: I love to travel and have visited over 70 different countries. I can offer help on visas, travel via air, train and car, all types of accommodation such as hotels, hostels, camping and Airbnb.

Now it's your turn. Write down ten subjects you can add value on, with a short description of your experience in that area. If you like, email me your 10 (my email contact is at the end of the book) and I will publish them on our

www.FiveYearsToFinancialFreedom.com or one of
our other blog sites.

EXERCISE 2: NETWORKING EVENTS

Write down six weekly events that you can commit to attending every week or every month (if the event is monthly):

1.

2.

3.

4.

5.

6.

CHAPTER 2:
Finding Your Value

IN THE PREVIOUS CHAPTER, YOU LEARNED HOW MANY people - when they first start networking - don't provide much value to the people who they meet. In fact, this isn't uncommon with people who have been networking for a while. So, what's the issue?

While there are some who purely see business events as a way to sell their product or service, they are in the minority. The reason why most people fail to provide value to others at networking events *isn't* because they're selfish or trying to force sales, it's because *they don't know their value.*

In this chapter, we will share with you three powerful techniques that will help you uncover your true value to others. We'll also share with you how to apply that newfound knowledge into your networking ability.

Your business persona consists of three key areas:

- Your knowledge

- Your skills

- Your network

These are the three areas that can provide huge value to the people you meet. Now if you *haven't* completed the exercises from Chapter 1, please do that now as the following exercises refine and build on it.

Exercise: Skills vs knowledge

A T THE END OF CHAPTER 1, WE ASKED YOU TO WRITE down ten subjects that you can offer an opinion on in any conversation. Let's refine and expand on those ten subjects:

1. Take a sheet of A4 paper and divide it into three sections

2. At the top of the first section write "My ten most valuable skills"

3. At the top of the second section write "Ten things I'm most knowledgeable about"

4. At the top of the third section write "Ten experienced people I know"

5. Under each section, simply list the first ten

items or people that spring to mind.

As in the Chapter 1 exercise example, don't feel pressure to keep it all strictly business. Depending on the situation and conversation, one of your most valuable skills could be "calming people down" or "being great at tennis".

Similarly, under the knowledge section, it doesn't need to all be "corporate machinations of a large IT firm"; you can also write things that you have a lot of personal experience with.

Finally, under the people section, don't restrict yourself to people in business, you could include your friends who run a five-a-side team, or who play in a band, or who love fishing.

The objective of the exercise isn't to make a CV (although you should include business related bits); it's to help you understand what areas you *know* you can help people with. If you can help someone with your skills, or teach someone with your knowledge, or connect them with someone that they'd like to meet, that's you providing *value*.

Unlocking the value of your knowledge

SO, YOU'VE GOT YOUR LIST OF TEN SUBJECTS that you're most knowledgeable about. Now, take another piece of paper and write down three bullet points that validate why you feel you're incredibly knowledgeable about the subject. Here are two examples from my own lists:

Comic books

- I've collected and read comic books for over a decade

- I'm at the point of nerdiness where I can tell you which issue of Uncanny X-men is my favourite (it's issue 157, *Phoenix Reborn*)

- The fact that I love comic books is so ingrained in my friends that they ask me to explain things in the recent surge of comic book films

Here's a more business-related example:

Copy writing:

- I've been writing for over 20 years, and have had countless articles published all over the web.

- I've earned a decent salary purely on my ability to write effectively.

- I've worked in a variety of editorial departments including journalistic, marketing, and academia.

The reason why it's good to mix "serious" knowledge with "fun" knowledge is that you never know what people need. As human beings, we tend to do business with people we like and can relate to. Building rapport and finding common ground to connect on provides a foundational boost to build a relationship.

It's very rare that you'll get business from someone at the first meeting. Again, you *need* to understand that networking is all about beginning relationships. You aren't selling your product, you aren't selling your services; you're selling yourself as someone who it would be great to connect and do business with.

The reason why you evidence your knowledge with three bullet points is so that you can explicitly understand *why* it is that you should consider yourself an expert on a topic. We spend so much of our lives (especially in the UK) focused on modesty that we devalue the things we *do* know a huge amount about.

If you don't feel you have expert knowledge in that area but have more knowledge than the average person, then still include the subject in the list. For example, I don't consider myself to be an expert in salsa because I network with the top dancers in the salsa arena. However, everyone outside of the salsa industry, consider me to be one of the best dancers they've met.

Unlocking the value of your skills

NOW, TAKE YOUR LIST OF 10 SKILLS that you feel are your most valuable, write them down on another sheet of A4, and write down three situations that best demonstrate the use of that skill. Again, here are some examples from my own life:

Leadership:

- I was the editor of a publication for which I had to make decisions about content direction, HR needs, budget allocation, and general day-to-day running of the publication.

- I taught adults and children. The key strength here was the variety of skills required to keep them involved, engaged and motivated. This strength also required you to understand each individual's strengths and weaknesses and leverage them to their benefit.

- Often when my friends need help they come to me for advice

Here's a more fun example:

Hosting parties:

- I was well-known among my friends as the "person who threw the best parties" (in my younger days)

- I've gate-crashed several parties, and by the end of the evening people were either trying to get selfies with me or saying to me "Thanks for throwing such a great party."

- I've MC'd a number of arts festivals, which taught me how to get everyone in a similar mood, and how to create a positive energetic atmosphere.

The purpose of this exercise is to prepare you for you to demonstrate your skills without saying "I'm a great leader" or "I host amazing parties".

There's an idea that's popular in any narrative medium: "Show, don't tell". If you're at a networking event and simply saying "I'm fantastic at..." people will just think that you're bragging or overcompensating.

However, when you share personal stories that *demonstrate* leadership skills (or of a great party host) then it *shows* people that you have a skill set that they may be interested in utilising.

When you list the various ways that you've demonstrated a certain skill, you also demonstrate several other valuable connected skills. For example, if you were a teacher and you wanted to share that you have leadership skills you would tell the story about how you used to teach children.

From that story, the person you are talking with, would also infer that you have patience, you are an effective communicator, and you can get up and speak well in front of a crowd.

The objective of this exercise is to help you understand and create fun stories that you can tell people at networking events. Fun stories that entertain others and, at the same time, show off your valuable skill set. Remember that stories are far more engaging and memorable than simply giving someone information.

NB: We have spent several thousands of hours networking. Everyone has a set of skills but not everyone has sufficient self-confidence to even write down what they are good at.

At a recent start-up event, a young man shared with me that he did not feel he had anything to offer anyone at the event. When I inquired what industry, he currently worked in, he shared that he worked in the catering industry and was a waiter.

Having worked in this industry, I know that good waiters happen to have extremely good social skills, the patience of saints, the ability to defuse potentially explosive customer situations, a good grasp of financial mechanics (i.e. resolving payment issues), an understanding of back pains, slippery floors, sexual harassment, repetitive strain injuries, and have to be incredibly organised when juggling the various customers and their orders.

If it helps, just do a brain dump of all the challenges you deal with in your life and job and you will quickly find out all the areas you have skills in.

Unlocking the value of your network

ALRIGHT, FINAL TASK! Take a sheet of A4 (20 points if you can guess what I'm going to say next).

Write down the ten most experienced people you know.

Under each name, write down three bullet points about what *value they provide to others.*

Again, it doesn't have to be just "business" value (although you should have a clear understanding about what it is they do); it could be a unique hobby, some way that they've given value to your life, or a skill that they excel at.

Here are a couple of my own examples (to prevent my friend's potential embarrassment I've changed the names):

Bobby Juggler:

- Programmer specialising in creating data visualisation and data sorting tools for financial institutions.

- Loves extreme sports, especially snowboarding and rock climbing.

- Fantastic at dissecting emotional problems and finding rational solutions.

Carly Beth:

- Musician, artist, and all around creative person.

- Speaks eloquently about philosophical topics like the nature of existence, truth, and purpose.

- Can surgically pinpoint when I'm being insensitive and this helps me sort myself out.

This exercise will help you on multiple levels. The first is in understanding potential business areas you can help your friends with. When someone is looking for people with specific skills, you already know the people in your list that are up to the task. The person you're networking with will appreciate the time you saved them in recruiting or speaking with an expert, and your friend will appreciate the referral.

The second is about personal motivation and confidence. It feels sublime to make a list of the people who you spend your time with and focus purely on how *amazing* they are. Here's a little technique. After listing the bullet points, show your friends the list you made about them. Ask them to verify the list and perhaps add other areas where they feel they could add value to others. Not only will they be flattered but you'll have deepened and strengthened your relationship with your friend.

Finally, one attitude that successful people value the *most* is loyalty. When you attend a business event and talk about how great your friends are *and* can give examples of why you enjoy spending time with them, it shows how *loyal* you are as a person.

Similarly, people who you network with, will unconsciously think "I'd love for someone to give testimonials about me like that." As a result, you will become a social magnet. The reason you will become a social magnet is that the best testimonial of anyone's capability is a third-party endorsement, and they will want *you* to be that third-party endorsement.

Chapter 2: Key Take-Aways:

FINDING YOUR VALUE

O NE COMMON THREAD, YOU MAY HAVE NOTICED throughout this chapter is that, when it comes to impressing people, you need to *show, not tell*. If you want people to understand the value that you can provide, it's ineffective to say, "I'm great at..."

Similarly, if you're talking about your knowledge or your existing network you can't simply say "I know loads about..." or "My friend is amazing at..." You *need* to tell a story that demonstrates that fact.

Before we end this chapter, here are several top tips on demonstrating value for each of the three categories:

Knowledge:

Arguably the easiest to convey: you just need to give good advice about *how* to do something effectively.

The advice you give gains power and credibility if you evidence *how* you gained this knowledge (i.e. tell the story of how, or why, you know what you do).

NEVER offer advice on a topic that you know nothing about, people respect that you know you're ignorant about a subject much more than someone who has read the answer on Google and talks about the subject as if you have experience.

In the property industry, we have met prolific forum posters, property authors, property community owners and people who talk knowledgeably about a subject but they've never ever done it.

I was sent a copy of property forum conversation where a prolific property poster is advising people against certain techniques on raising capital. After days of conversation it turned out that the property poster had never ever raised angel capital and was simply using the conversation to advertise their property community. Outside of the community this person's credibility took a massive nosedive.

Skills:

Tell stories that demonstrate *when* you used the skill in question. Make the story engaging and interesting, and weave the skill into the story.

Nobody likes a bragger. A feature of the story could be that you were "the top salesman of [company]" but don't make that the focus.

With that said, if you can use statistics to back up a bold claim (or it's been publicised online) you should share about it. Be sure to share your *method* for achieving those results.

Network:

Your objective is to connect two people with similar interests, regardless of whether it will benefit you. Putting two people together is a great win-win for everyone involved and will pay you great dividends.

Think carefully about *who* you talk about; if you wouldn't do business with them, don't recommend them to others. If you can't think of ten people to include on your list, then just have a shorter list. The importance of quality over quantity cannot be emphasized enough. Conversely, if you have been on this planet for three plus decades, it is a real testimony of your networking skills, if you have fifty plus quality people in your list.

NEVER bad-mouth at a public event. If you meet with someone privately, and they specifically mention someone you've had negative dealings with, then *objectively* tell them the outcome and let them make a decision for themselves.

FINDING YOUR VALUE EXERCISE

TAKE A SHEET OF A4 PAPER AND DIVIDE IT INTO THREE sections.

- At the top of section one write "My ten most valuable skills".

- Write down three bullet points that validate why you feel you're incredibly knowledgeable about each of the ten subjects.

- At the top of section two list "ten things I'm most knowledgeable about."

- Write down three situations that best demonstrate the use of each of the ten skills

- At the top of section three list "ten experienced people I know".

- Write down three bullet points about what value each of your ten experienced friends provide to others

CHAPTER 3:
Conversation Mastery

IN THE LAST CHAPTER, YOU UNCOVERED HOW TO UNLOCK YOUR VALUE TO OTHERS. When you understand how amazing and valuable you are to others, the seeds of greatness within you is given extra fertiliser. If you haven't yet understood your value, please redo the last chapters exercises. This knowledge alone will give you confidence to share with others and also to leave a conversation when someone does not understand your value.

One uncomfortable situation at a networking event is when you are trapped with and talking to a bore. Someone who you don't think you can help in any shape or form, and yet due to societal norms you cannot simply leave the conversation.

There are many reasons why this person is such a bore. It could be their nerves, pressure from work, poor training, or a general lack of social ability. Nevertheless, being forced to spend time with these people is a waste of your time *and* theirs. Later in this book you'll learn several tried and tested methods for exiting conversations that result in a win-win.

An unfortunate aspect of learning a new skill is that you're going to start off being *bad* at it. Remember that person we mentioned previously?... that could be *you!* From my stories in Chapter 1, you can see the bore has been me at certain times of my life.

Remember, the skill you are developing is the skill to present your value in an engaging and charismatic way. Now this chapter *won't* teach you how to walk into a room and have Tom Cruise levels of charisma (we do offer coaching if that's what you're after); but you will learn how to connect with and hold someone's attention!

Sadly, even after everything you learn from this book, you will still have some bad conversations. That's just the nature of socialisation. When people begin to attend business events, these "bad" conversations can have a negative impact on you and potentially decrease your morale and motivation. In this chapter, you will gain from five techniques we've learned from experience to move forward, even after negative conversations.

What people don't want to hear

THERE ARE SOME SUBJECTS THAT ARE INAPPROPRIATE to talk about at networking events, and could potentially get you into trouble.

Here are the top five taboo subjects you *shouldn't* talk about at any business event:

- Politics (unless it is your political party event)

- Religion (unless it is a religious event such as going to church)

- Sex (unless the event is specifically about sex)

- Drug use

- Attractiveness of other attendees

The subjects on that list needn't be said, but you'd be surprised at how often people share their opinions about those topics. It's not that the topics themselves are inherently bad, but people have very personal and sometimes emotive opinions on these subjects. As a result, you may accidentally alienate a great contact.

Remember the purpose of networking is to start relationships and create deep connections, *not* to "win" conversations. Talking about politics or religion will often create barriers between people, which is the opposite of the purpose of this book.

Now we've covered the taboos, let's get on with the *boring*. Certain common questions will create boring answers. You *will not* be able to escape boring "everyone-always-asks-these" questions. So, what you need to do is come up with exciting *answers*. Similarly, when you ask people these questions, expect a response that people will give a standard but un-engaging response to. Later on in this book you'll learn how to ask better questions which will produce a more engaging reply and a stronger connection. Here are the top five "standard networking questions."

- What do you do?

- Where are you based?

- What did you think of the speaker?

- How did you get here? (This one always baffles me)

- What do you think of the weather?

Here's what people are really trying to understand about you when they ask you these questions:

"WHAT DO YOU DO?"

When someone asks you this question they're trying to understand your role. To answer it in an engaging and interesting way, take them through a recent project that you were a part of. Be outcome focused and tell them what it is that you and your team were trying to achieve.

"WHERE ARE YOU BASED?"

When you are asked this question, the person is looking for something both of you may have in common. This is a good thing: they're attempting to build rapport with you. Your answer should be the most famous location near you i.e. the biggest city closest to you/most well-known.

If you don't live near an iconic area, answer with the place you're from and immediately offer what you like most about the area, i.e. "There's a fantastic Italian restaurant" or "You can go on some fantastic walks." By sharing things that interest you, the other person can expand the conversation if they so wish.

"WHAT DID YOU THINK OF THE SPEAKER?"

So, the reason why people ask you this question is that it's more interesting than asking someone what they do. Rather than sharing your opinions on the speaker, share about what you learned and your key takeaways from the talk. Then ask the other person what they found most exciting about the event or what they learned.

"HOW DID YOU GET HERE?"

Seriously, I have *no idea* why people insist on asking this question. Potentially, it's asking you about your wealth status, but that may be reading too deeply into it. The trick here is to quickly pivot the conversation to another topic, for example: "I took the train, and I read this news article about... isn't that incredible?"

"WHAT DO YOU THINK OF THE WEATHER?"

This question is the nuclear bomb of small talk. Whatever the real reason for the question, steer the conversation into an area, you feel will be of more interest to both of you. In your response to the weather question, share an activity that the weather has enabled you to do, even if the weather is bad, e.g. "Thankfully the rain meant that I had to stay indoors and finish my presentation."

The closest insight given for the use of the weather question comes from this personal story. A customer took a group of us writers to a Luxembourg event. I remember asking the group, the purpose of the questions "What do you think about the weather?" or the question "The rain is terrible isn't it?" After much discussion, the conclusion is that is a cultural question designed to see if someone wanted to carry on with a conversation or not.

If you get a one-worded answer such as "Fine" or "Yes", then the person is not interested in proceeding with any kind of conversation with you.

If the answer to the question has more than a few words such as "It's amazing and I've enjoyed getting some sunlight..." or "The rain has been quite refreshing..." Then the person is interested in having a conversation with you.

NB: *Each of your answers to the standard questions should give the person you are talking with additional hooks to progress the conversation further. As in the weather explanation above, a succinct or one-word answer to any of the questions such as "What do you do?" or "Where are you from?" will more than likely signal to the other person that the conversation is over.*

Before we move on, here are some general tips about what to avoid talking about:

Jargon: Corporate jargon doesn't make you seem smart, and neither does it save time.

Job titles: Due to the top-down hierarchy of most large businesses, most titles denote a *rank* rather than a *role*. Similarly, a "business analyst" at one company may have a very different day-to-day role than one at another firm.

Negativity: Don't bring negativity about anyone or anything to a networking event. At best, people don't want to engage with a downer. At worst, your moaning and complaining could get back to the people who you're complaining about.

What people do want to hear?

OBVIOUSLY, THIS BEGS THE QUESTION, what *do* people want to hear? This question isn't very useful; a far better question is "What interests people?" What are the two most popular mediums for media consumption? At a guess, I'd assume that it's television and radio, i.e. songs and stories. Songs are all about expressing an emotion (usually related to love) and popular stories are about *drama*.

When we talk with people we want to hear about emotions, we want to listen to stories, and we want to know about *conflict* and resolutions. So, to take your social magnetism to the next level, one engaging way to answer a question at an event is to *tell a story*. "But I'm not a good story teller!" I hear you cry. Don't worry, here are the three key elements of a compelling story:

1. No problem

2. Problem

3. Solution

Here's an example of this framework in action, answering the question "What do you do?"

No problem: I used to be an English Teacher in South Korea, which was really fulfilling as I got to see the progress in the kids I taught.

Problem: But I felt that I could be doing *more*; I saw that people in South Korea were really struggling with their financial situation.

Solution: So, I started Five Years to Financial Freedom to provide high-value advice to property investors, entrepreneurs, and people who want to achieve financial freedom.

This is a far more effective answer than "I work in education". It gives the listener more information (or conversational hooks) to expand the conversation further by either asking further questions or sharing their own opinions. Use the story telling technique with the question about how you reached your current position (even if you've been doing it for *ages*). When you use the technique, you'll invite a lot more questions about yourself.

Now did you see the embedded emotional words in the story? "Fulfilling", "progress", "struggling", "achieve", and "freedom" are all highly emotive words. These types of words engage the more primal parts of our psyche and *encourage* us to pay attention to what the speaker is saying.

On that note, it is worth buying a thesaurus just to learn more emotionally charged words. One of my positions involved being a content marketeer. In this position, I had to write attention-grabbing headlines all day long which helped me develop my knowledge about which words were more effective in getting people's attention. For example, "ecstatic" is far more effective than "happy", "distraught" is more emotive than "sad", and "serene" is more descriptive than "quiet". Think about the emotive words that you use, and expand your vocabulary to use powerful emotional words.

When you engage with people emotionally you stimulate their decision-making process, and the only decision they need to make that evening is: "Would I like to do business and connect further with this person?" Thankfully, due to the quirks in human psychology we will choose the person who makes us feel emotionally connected over the person who makes us feel logically connected.

Tell people what you *actually do*

I KNOW THAT WE'VE ALREADY DISCUSSED THIS TWICE, but you need to be telling people what you *actually* do. Don't tell them about your job title. Don't tell them what was written on your job description. Tell people what you *actually* do!

People will ask you this question all the time, so prepare a great answer in advance. In this section, you will learn three response frameworks that will intrigue people and captivate their interest. These three response frameworks are the underdog story, the project leader and the elevator pitch.

THE UNDERDOG STORY

The underdog story uses the same story telling framework discussed in the previous section. Use this when you want to demonstrate your determination, grit, and tenacity. The lovely benefit of the underdog story is that it showcases your ability and if told correctly will invite further comments, because your answer will demonstrate key personality traits to overcome the hardship. Here is the underdog story in action:

Them: "What do you do?"

You: "I used to work for a publication that was losing money. Every single month the publication profit margin would be less and less, things were looking *dire*. Six months later, after some hard HR decisions, and a hell of a lot of hard work, I'm now the editor of the UK's third largest (profitable) B2B tech magazine."

You can see from the answer how several parts of

someone's skill set has been demonstrated within that story *and* how the story engaged the listener with emotive language.

THE PROJECT LEADER

The essential idea behind this framework is to share about objectives, skills, and outcomes that you and your team are aiming for. the purpose of the project leader framework is to give the listener a better idea of what your role actually involves. Let's take the example of a person with a role or title of "data manager."

Them: "What do you do?"

You: "I'm in data management, which is actually quite exciting. Last week my team and I were tasked with providing our sales people easier access to five years' worth of sales data. This sales data would enable our sales people to better research our client's needs. After a few days of coding, our sales team are now able to ask the database questions like 'What item sells the most during the summer months?' or 'Which item has consistently increased in popularity over the past three years? Or in which country do the male population over the age of 44 buy the most of our top-end products?'"

Here you've demonstrated that you can explain complex work in a simple way, shown that you understand *how* and *why* you complete tasks, *and* shown that you value the individual roles that people play in a company.

THE ELEVATOR PITCH

If you work for a company, you should *always* be looking for a better job. Unfortunately, loyalty to a corporation is no longer as highly prized as it used to be. Some corporations even have processes that actively look at outsourcing and culling.

Always be on the lookout for bigger and better projects to be a part of. The elevator pitch framework is a great framework to use when you want a promotion, you want a new job, you have an opportunity to sell a product, or you wish to promote your department within the company.

The thought process behind the elevator pitch framework is to imagine yourself as a company that's looking for investment, and to pitch that company to potential "investors". That's what hiring a potential employee really is about, an investment. It is taking a risk by paying for something that you expect to bring you a greater return.

The elevator pitch consists of the answers to three questions:

- What problem do you solve?

- What do you want to do?

- Why do you want to do it?

Here's an example:

Them: "What do you do?"

You: "Have you ever wanted a product set that everyone is a fan of?"

Them: "Yes, who doesn't?"

You: Well our customers love our product set for the security, the colour co-ordination, the great comments from their friends and neighbours so much that many have in fact become brand advocates. With five years' experience and hundreds of positive customer testimonials, my role is to imagine and create those products. May I look at one of your products and see what I could design?"

It's clear that you are passionate in product design, have a passion for it and want to add value by sharing how you see the other person's product suite.

Tell them what you're excited about

NO MATTER THE QUESTION ASKED, answer the question by sharing what you're passionate about, and explain *why*. Even answering the basic "How are you doing?" using this method demonstrates you as an engaged individual. For example:

Them: "How are you?"

You: "Really good. I just read in the news about <name a product or service you are interested in here>! Can you believe what they've done <name how

they've positively or negatively transformed the product here>?"

When you answer questions passionately, you stand out from the crowd, and give the listener more information about yourself. You've also steered the conversation to things that interest you, and given the other person conversational hooks that they can use to further the conversation.

This excited framework is useful when asked *small-talky* questions, like:

- How are you?

- Enjoying the weather?

- How was the traffic?

On that note, you should relate the thing that you're enthusiastic about to the question, otherwise it seems too much like a non-sequitur (which it is). For example, if someone asks, "How was the traffic?" and you say "Fantastic! I just read in the news about ...," this suggests to the other person that you didn't listen to their question.

A far better response to "How was the traffic?" would be "Well you know how the A309 can be on a Tuesday. However, I did listen to this fantastic audio book while I was caught up in the traffic, it talked about..." and from there start discussing something that you find fascinating.

Ensure that your answer to the question makes sense in the context of the question. Your added comment about whatever you're passionate about needs to seem like a "oh, that reminds me..." rather than a "I need to talk about this".

As your social magnetism expands and you get better at answering questions you may fall into a conversational pitfall. Once you get good at being charming and engaging you may accidentally dominate fun and lively discussions. Think about your ideal outcome for the networking evening, and temper yourself accordingly.

For example, when looking for a new partner, take a backseat in conversations and watch how others interact with each other. Watching and listening will give you a better idea of who the other person is. The people with the most social magnetism tend to listen more than most. However, they also know when to speak and steer a conversation into areas that are beneficial to everyone present.

Ask them emotionally charged questions

ULTIMATELY, YOU *SHOULDN'T* BE DOING MOST OF THE talking. Remember the goal is to connect with and add value to someone. So, find out as much as you can about someone in a non-intrusive manner. Non-intrusive means that if you are likely to ask personal questions because for example you are a financial consultant or a doctor then ask for their permission before you ask your question. For example, I hope you don't mind but may I ask you a personal question about your finances as I think I can probably double your current income but would like to understand the starting point. No matter what you're trying to achieve, people will be far more engaged (and you will be too) if you can connect with them on an emotional level.

Emotional connections doesn't mean you need to be crying in each other's arms at the end of the evening, nor does it require you to share your innermost thoughts about private matters. It simply means that you need to engage in emotionally focused talk rather than informationally focused talk.

Similarly, you should keep things professional, but add some emotion to the standard questions people ask strangers. Have a look at the information vs emotion table.

INFORMATIONAL	EMOTIONAL
What do you do?	What's your favourite thing about your job?
How are you?	What's the most exciting thing that's happened to you today?
How long have you worked in [industry]?	What drives you to be the best [job title] in [industry]?
What are the current trends in [industry]?	What are the most surprising trends in [industry]?
Where are you from?	What was the best part of growing up?

One useful aspect of this technique is that it provides you with insightful intelligence on a potential business partner's or investor's mindset and motivations. Let's analyse an answer to "What's your favourite thing about your job?" Let's assume they say "Nothing, my job's boring"; what is implied about this person from their answer?

They lack motivation to change their position.

You could also infer from this that they prefer to choose security over freedom, and are therefore risk averse.

They find the negative even when asked about the positive.

Possible chance of a victim complex, as they can't see how their job is valuable to the company or business overall.

They don't wish to talk with you.

Naturally, I could just be reading too much into this, and I would need to see their body language, facial expression and listen to their intonation, to better understand them as a person. With that said, the language, tone, and chosen words all play a part in revealing someone's personality. Think about *why* people say the things they do, and you'll be able to read people much better.

In addition, be conscious of how *you* answer questions and approach conversations. Once you understand *why* you say the things you do, you'll be well on the way to self-mastery... but that's a topic for another book.

Finally, if someone responds negatively to your question, try to understand why. A great follow up to the answer "my job is boring" would be "What are the three most boring things about your job?" You'll gain knowledge and ideas; people's pain points are far easier to leverage into business ideas.

Never underestimate the power of flattery

THE REASON FOR THE PREVIOUS EXAMPLE is because many people think that their job is boring. When we work with a product, service, or team or a daily basis, we become de-sensitised to how much knowledge and experience we have in that field.

An illustration of this desensitisation was a bar conversation I once had with a friend. In the bar, I asked him if he'd like to go for dinner the next week. He told me that he couldn't because he was out of town on business, then he began to complain that his job was "uninteresting", "tedious", and "boring".

My friend fixes helicopters for a living!

The truth is that every role is an essential part of how a company operates, and you can help remind them of that. When we meet new people, we don't remember what they say as much as we remember how they made us *feel*.

By taking an interest in their job, and how they operate, they'll share so much knowledge with you. They'll tell you which programs are useful for their role, how to spot someone who isn't doing their job properly, things you need to be paying for, things you absolutely *don't* need to pay for.

When they share intimate aspects of their lives do show your appreciation using a sincere compliment.

People may find the compliment refreshing but don't overdo it (even if you mean it) and don't make the compliment up, otherwise you'll be perceived as false and insincere.

Also, simple compliments are great for ice breakers. If you're worried about being unprofessional in a "business environment", you needn't be, just look at these dos and don'ts:

DO:

- Compliment items and processes that they have control over, i.e. clothes, jewellery, shoes, hair colour (only if it's obvious), accessories

- Focus on the character trait that the object you're complimenting shows off. For example, "Nice briefcase! It gives you a suave edge", or "Excellent choice of suit, you look ready for action"

- Be specific. For example, say *what* you like and *why* you like it. If you're talking to the speaker of an event don't say "Thanks for the speech", say, "Thanks for the speech, I found the bit about... really useful"

DON'T:

- Compliment things that people can't control: things like height, attractiveness, or eye colour.

- Compliment everyone in a group, just the first person you talk to. The others will hear your compliment and agree with you, and people will know that you're a nice person. If you compliment everyone you'll seem needy.

- Lie. Ever. Only compliment someone on something that you like about them

Listen!

ONE OF THE GREATEST CONVERSATIONAL GIFTS you can give someone is to actively listen to them. It's not often that people actively listen to what someone is saying. There is so much to being a good listener that it would take another book to go through all the techniques. Being a good listener alone, will magnify your social magnetism tremendously.

Being a great listener takes far more practice than being a great speaker because of how nuanced human communication is. Here are ten tips to help you improve your ability to listen:

1. Concentrate on what they're saying, remove other thoughts from your mind.

2. Be still. Moving around, shuffling, or looking at other things such as your phone will suggest that you're not listening to the speaker.

3. Nod and smile as they speak, use non-verbal cues to show that you're listening.

4. Wait! If you have a question, allow the other person to finish before asking it.

5. Don't inject your personal prejudice into conversations with strangers.

6. Imagine yourself in their position, seek to understand the context of what they're saying.

7. Look for how all the pieces of information that they're giving you fit together. Although most conversations contain informational content, people share a lot more about themselves if you can imagine the bigger picture.

8. If you feel the urge to speak, *stop it!* When you start out, try writing any thoughts and questions you have on a piece of paper.

9. *How* someone says something is as important as *what* they say.

10. *Use active listening.* Active listening paraphrases what the speaker is saying and signals to them that you are listening. For

example, if the speaker shares with you several benefits of writing your own book. Reflect what they say back to them.

"So if I can recap, what you are telling me is that if I was to write my own book, I would get more indirect business as the book will demonstrate my authority in this area...."

These tips are designed to help you focus on what someone is trying to say. Rather than simply cognitively recognise the words, you need to understand *why* the words are being said and whether there is an underlying message. A good listener is about understanding the truth behind the words rather than just hearing the words.

Chapter 3 Key take-aways

ATTENTION IS SOMETHING YOU GIVE

IN THIS CHAPTER, WE'VE BUILT ON YOUR PERSONAL VALUE and the skills and knowledge of your friends to build a foundation and increase your confidence to master the art of conversation.

Conversation mastery is about giving value to others.

To give value, when you enter a conversation with someone you need to make it about *them*. The benefits of allowing someone (and encouraging them) to speak about themselves is truly what makes people think you are interesting, because people rarely listen.

Think about it. When was the last time someone sat down with you and just... listened? With no judgement, no interruptions, no opinions offered or to redirect the conversation about *themselves*?

A gift of your full attention to someone for even five minutes is a hugely powerful gift to give. If you can give someone five minutes of emotionally charged conversation about the things that they love, the things they enjoy, and the things that they want to achieve, that is something that people will crave. If you can share something honest and truthful about yourself that brings a bit of novelty and joy to someone's mundane evening, that's something that will hold someone's attention.

Here is a recap on the five things you need to know about getting, and holding, someone's attention:

Talk about projects not titles: Give someone insight into your actual day-to-day life. It will help them connect with you at a deeper level.

Talk with passion: No matter the question, use the opportunity to talk about something you enjoy, or are excited about.

Ask them about their passion: Whenever you ask a question add an emotional twist.

Everyone is valuable: We often forget how important we are; remind others of how important they are.

Listen: Instead of simply hearing someone's words, try to understand them. Listen to what they don't say as well as what they do say.

Chapter 3 Exercises

WHERE ARE YOU FROM EXERCISE

Write down your answer to the question for "How did you end up living where you live today?" This is your answer for when people ask you "Where are you from?"

HOW ARE YOU EXERCISE

Write down an answer to the question "What happened to make you feel the way you're currently feeling?" Use the style of answer you've written down to answer the question "How are you?"

WHAT DO YOU DO EXERCISE

Write down your answer to the question "Why do you

do what you are doing today?" Give people your answer when they ask you "What do you do?"

Remember to include these components in your answer.

- What problem do you solve?

- What do you want to do?

- Why do you want to do it?

ACTIVE LISTENING EXERCISE

Write down five ways in which other people make you feel listened to and heard:

1.
2.
3.
4.
5.

Now incorporate all five into your conversations with people.

CHAPTER 4:
When Conversations Go Wrong

THE CORE REASON MOST PEOPLE DREAD NETWORKING events is because of one simple fact: You have to talk to strangers. This terrifies us! There are many different explanations for this; some argue that it's how incessantly "Don't talk to strangers" was drilled into us as children. Others feel that it's because modern technology and all its on-line communication has deadened our ability to connect on a face-to-face level.

Whatever the reason, we do know that there is a certain amount of stress related to meeting new people. Perhaps this stress stems from humanity's fear of rejection. The crippling possibility that when you go to talk with people they might not like you.

And indeed, they might not! However, there is no easy cure for this affliction. Your fear of rejection is something you're going to have to deal with. Dealing with the fear of rejection is a huge challenge that you must address if you want to jump start your business and help it grow exponentially.

One solution is to practice and to jump right into talking with people. In this chapter, you will learn five key mindset traits to build your resilience and confidence. Once you change the way you think, your perception will change. Once your perception changes you will overcome your fear, and start meeting amazing people.

Everyone has been in your shoes

AT SOME POINT IN THEIR LIVES, *EVERYONE* in the room was scared of talking to new people. Even the person you see sweeping around the room talking to everyone and leaving people with huge smiles on their faces had to *learn* that skill.

Similarly, everyone who is an effective networker has a lot of sympathy for the newcomers. They understand how it can be when you first start out. As a result, experienced networkers are extremely accommodating and make it a point to include newbies and shy people into conversations.

One excellent example of an "introducer", is Marian Gadzik. At time of writing, Marian Gadzik is the European director of StartUp Grind, the largest networking event for tech start-ups in the UK.

Marian makes it his job to ensure everyone at every event connects with other people. You will be constantly amazed at how Marian retains in his head, the skills and jobs each of the 100 plus attendees and the skilful way in which Marian portrays the strength of each attendee to other people at his events.

Experienced networkers suggest that if you feel nervous, admit your nervousness/shyness to people when it comes to networking, and that you feel out of your comfort zone.

When I began covering technical business events for a magazine, I knew nothing about networking and started conversations with: "Hey guys, what's the most useful piece of advice someone's given you about networking?" (The answers were mostly, "learn how to exit conversations", "talk to as many people as you can", and "offer value first".)

When it comes to learning a new skill, most of us want to run before we can walk. We judge ourselves by the best people using that skill, which can lead to frustration when we don't perform at the same level. When you start out, just focus on getting better at the skill of networking and connecting; ask questions like:

- What do you think people are most interested in talking about at these events?

- What are your biggest networking pain points at these events?

- How can I better my networking skills?

Asking the above questions, in addition to the questions about the event topics will give others the opportunity to help you develop a skill that they had to work out for themselves. If instead of being experienced, they are new to networking themselves, you will make your fellow newbies feel far more included, knowing that others at the event feel exactly as they do.

Most conversations are scripted

AFTER ATTENDING A FEW NETWORKING EVENTS you'll realise that most conversations have already been mentally written. Experienced networkers tend to slip into "networking autopilot", giving canned responses to canned questions over and over. You've got your "engaging answer about what I do", then you've got your "30 second pitch about my start-up/business/project", and you've got your "funny business story to build rapport".

Use this to your advantage.

Networking is unlike the "real world" where people can instinctually tell when you've slipped into autopilot. Create a question-inviting, emotionally engaging, attention-grabbing response to the questions you *know* are going to get asked. Plan and practise your responses to those questions.

Use the Informational to Emotional table in the previous chapter to create an engaging response to a question. For example, when someone asks, "Where are you from?" share your answer for "What was your favourite thing about growing up?"

Prepare for an upcoming event by creating questions that rarely get asked at events (see the previous chapter for ideas). Write them on your phone and, if you feel nervous, take a quick peek. Over time you'll learn what works and what doesn't.

For example, a great question that almost *never* gets asked is, "If you had to choose one task to do all day, what would it be and why?" It's a great question because it teaches the other person something about themselves, *and* gives you an idea of their skill set and desires for the future.

A bad example of this (in my experience) is, "If you were the boss, how would you change the way the company is run?" I thought it'd be a fun thing to ask, but it turns conversations into a complain-a-thon. Similarly, it positions you as someone who doesn't like authority, or thinks that they can do a job better than everyone else.

Once you understand how automated people's responses are, you can create more perceptive conversations and - over time - better understand their motivations. There is a balancing act between being inquisitive and focusing *way too much* on a facet of someone's story. Remember it is a conversation, and it is a conversation between people who do not necessarily know each other so:

- Ensure you don't ask too many personal questions until you know the person better.

- Ensure it is a conversation and not a one-way interrogator/prisoner situation which is all too common in newbies.

- Ensure that the conversation is a dialogue so if you are talking too much – stop and invite comments from others.

- Ensure you understand that every conversation is a lesson in networking.

Every conversation is a lesson

LET'S TAKE AN EXAMPLE OF THE SKILL of playing the violin. If someone has never tried to play the violin, you wouldn't get annoyed at them if they could not play the violin. Similarly, if they've only spent a few hours learning the instrument, you'd forgive them for hitting a few bum notes.

Networking is just like learning a new skill. Each time you muster the courage to talk to someone you're practising that skill, so don't worry about making mistakes because you're still learning. Bear in mind that I'm *not* saying that the mistakes don't matter.

Create a conversation analysis framework for yourself and look at interactions that you have with people objectively. After conversations, mentally go over what happened and think about why people reacted in a certain way. For example:

When I said "[phrase]" the other person's body weight shifted. What does this mean? And why did it happen?

How do I deal with new people entering the conversation without ruining the flow of my story?

When I asked "[question]?" the conversation changed to becoming more informational. How can I adapt the question to keep it emotional (or vice versa)?

This conversational framework will help you build experiential knowledge about what does and doesn't work well. As an added benefit, when you begin to use this conversational framework, you will become less frustrated because each time you fail to hit your goal, you will see it as a positive learning experience.

People spend months, years, and decades to become an expert. The skill of networking is no different. Think about conversations as lessons. After each conversation think about what you could have done better/what that lesson taught you.

It's not personal

AT A BUSINESS NETWORK EVENT PEOPLE AREN'T really being themselves, they're being their business persona. In the same way that you may behave differently at work than you do at home, people behave differently at business network events than they do at a social event such as a party.

Remember everyone has an ideal outcome of the event you're attending. Some people are on a fact-finding mission, some people are looking to start business relationships, and some people are there to sell their product.

If someone doesn't want to speak to you it's not about them thinking that you're not good enough, or that they don't like you as a person. It's about *them* wanting to achieve the goals that they or their company have set for that event.

In the same manner, you'll run into plenty of people who you can't provide value to, or who you don't think you can do business with. Not because they're bad people but because they're not the kind of person that you're looking to meet that evening.

When you react to conversations that end in a way that you feel hurt by, take a step back. Look at the context of what just happened, and think about all the reasons that they may have ended the conversation with you. There are two possible outcomes: the first is that you learn something about your communication style; and the second is that you see what was going on with them and learn how to read people better.

Remember that when a conversation doesn't go the way you imagined, it's not a reflection on who you are. The person you're talking to may already have someone who can do what you'd like to do for them, they may not need your service at this time, and they may even be able to do what you do themselves.

Exiting a conversation (without anyone feeling bad)

THERE ARE TIMES WHEN YOU'LL BE CHATTING to someone and not be able to offer any value to them. You can't connect them with any of your friends because they don't need those skills that your friends provide. You can't share your expertise with them because they already have sufficient expertise in whatever area, and they've already got someone with your skillset. So, what do you do?

Realise that in this situation, you're wasting each other's valuable time. At this point, it's important to end the conversation ASAP so you both can find people who you can provide value to. Here are three tried and tested methods for exiting conversations without anyone's feelings being hurt.

It's also important to note that if you're in a group and want to leave, simply smile, say "It was great meeting you guys" and walk away. These techniques are for one-on-one conversations.

HAAAAAAAAAAAAVE YOU MET....

With a title that may or may not have been taken from a popular sitcom, the "Haaaaaaaaaaaaaave you met...?" method is where you introduce a stranger to the person you're talking to.

As your chatting simply grab a passer-by and introduce your conversational partner.

After you've made your introductions all you need to do is, smile, say "it was great meeting you guys" and walk away. The reason why this is an effective method is that it stops the other person awkwardly standing by themselves, a feeling that I wouldn't wish on anyone.

THE THIRST QUENCHER

With this technique, you'll need your eagle eyes peeled. Is their drink empty? Are there snacks that they may want? Use the environment to your advantage.

At a natural break, ask your partner that you're going to get a drink and if they'd also like one. Then exit. The idea here is that by the time you've gone to get a drink and come back, they'll already be conversing with a new person. At which point; smile, "it was great to meet you guys", etc.

You're providing value to this person by getting them something, and showing this person that people will chat to them!

For a sure fire, get-out-of-the-conversation-free card, combine this technique with the "Haaaaaaaaaaaave you met?" method. Be sure to get both of the conversationalists drinks!

HONEST BOMB

If you've got the mettle (or don't like the other methods), you can drop an "Honest bomb". All you have to do is say "Hey! My goal is to talk to five new people this evening, can you help me out?" And take them with you to find other people to talk to.

Once they're settled into another conversation... well you know the exit procedure by now.

THE EXITING GOLDEN RULE

There are many other techniques that you can use to exit conversations and you'll want to try a few different ones before you find one that *fits*. However, it's important to remember these golden rules of networking:

- Don't leave someone standing by themselves

- Do your best to help people feel comfortable

- Be kind

As long as you can exit conversations by adhering to those three rules, you'll have a great time! Except when people – and this is rare – when people are *rude*.

Rudeness is a filter

IN ALL MY YEARS GOING TO NETWORKING EVENTS, I can list on one hand how many people have been rude or offensive at a networking event. However, when it does (rarely) happen it can shake your confidence and ruin the rest of the evening for you.

[Nate] I remember being at a trade show and I saw this product that looked cool so I went up to the booth and started chatting with the person at the booth. It was going well at first – he was enthusiastically telling me all about the product. Then he asked me, "What do you do?" I told him that I was a writer... he then refused to speak to me. He completely shut down, the smile on his face dropped, and he started to look everywhere but my direction.

I was mortified.

I was actually mega-concerned for him and asked, "Are you OK?" He looked me dead in the eye and nodded. We then stared at each other for a solid 10 seconds (which is a long time to stare at a stranger). At that point I said, "Thanks for your help" and walked away.

At the time I was rattled, my mind was flooded with "Who does he think he is?!" and "How dare he speak to me like that?!" After I'd sat down and had a drink of water I realised that when someone is rude it's useful to me. When someone is offensive to you then you 100 per cent know that you won't be able to do any sort of business with them.

Businesses are all about relationships with people. If a buyer has a great relationship with an existing supplier, then it is extremely unlikely that they will change to a cheaper competitor. When people in each of the businesses enjoy working together then they are likely to stay together. There are many hidden costs created by bad relationships, for example emotional costs of arguing, time wasted due to poor communication, and the inevitable cost of shifting to a new supplier.

If someone is rude to you, you should be grateful as they've saved you the time and energy of having a conversation and potentially doing business with them.

Chapter 4 Key take-aways

YOU'RE ALREADY A NETWORKING EXPERT

A T THE POINT IN YOUR LIFE WHEN YOU BEGIN to attend networking events, you've probably already had hundreds of thousands of interactions with other human beings. Realistically, networking is just a niche of human interaction, and follows the same rules.

However, unlike the majority of conversations you'll have in life, people at networking events are actually *interested* in hearing about your job and what you do at work. If you're still not convinced here are our five techniques again:

Everyone has gone through the same journey: If you're new to networking people will understand and the majority will look to help you improve.

You don't need to think on the fly: Most of our responses have already been generated, which means you can practise even when you're not at events and put a plan in place.

Allow yourself to be a pupil: Think analytically about each conversation, and figure out what you learned from each one.

It's not about you: Networking is essentially a "skills market", where people trade in abilities. You may simply not have the ability they're looking for.

Embrace rudeness: If someone is rude to you (and that's unlikely) they've saved you the most precious resource of all: time.

Chapter 4 Exercises

CONVERSATIONAL EXERCISE

Have three 15-minute conversations with people you don't know well. At the end of each conversation. Use your own version of a conversational framework to think about how you could have made the conversation go more smoothly.

Write down three things that would have improved the conversation and anything you will avoid doing in future conversations.

CHAPTER 5:
Foundations of Amazing Follow-ups

A S WE'VE REPEATEDLY SAID, *networking is just a first impression.* The true value of networking unveils itself once you convert those you meet at an event into people you have relationships with.

Ironically, people find attendance at a networking event most difficult when it's actually the follow-up that is most tricky. Think about all the friends you have on Facebook, now think about the friends who you call on a regular basis, and now think about the friends who you spend time with regularly. Think about how much *time* and *energy* it takes to maintain all those relationships. You have to follow the same - if not better strategy - to maintain all your business contacts.

But fear not! In this chapter, you will learn how to build and maintain quality contacts, and transform them from acquaintance to customer, supplier, or collaborator. You'll also learn several systems and techniques to make the process as simple and as fun as possible

The things to focus on
at the event itself

AT A NETWORKING EVENT, IF YOU FEEL YOU CAN HELP someone, take their business card *and* add them on LinkedIn/Facebook. Even in today's modern age, people ignore the Facebook of Business when they're out meeting people.

The reason you both add the other person on LinkedIn *and* take their business card is to help you build your own database of email addresses, phone numbers, and responsibilities. This database will ensure that you don't waste time connecting with the wrong people.

NB: Get a business card scanner app for your phone. This scanner will save you a huge amount of time, and you won't need to manually input the data into whatever database system you use.

At an event, focus on building a sense of the character of the people you have conversations with, rather than selling them on your business. There are two reasons for this. The first is that selling someone on your business is a bit too forward when you don't know this person and whether you connect with them. You don't want to commit to something that you don't want to do. The second is that business planning requires intense informational thinking, when an event is simply a gateway to set up a meeting where there will be less noise and interruptions.

One goal when you meet someone at an event is to answer the question: *Do I want to continue a relationship with this person?*

Similarly, your follow-up (or post event) goal should be: *How do I now create a lasting relationship with the people I met?*

Event follow-up strategy

TO ANSWER THE ABOVE QUESTIONS, USE YOUR OWN version of the follow-up strategy we will now outline. The day after the event, send the people you had a good connection with a message. The message may be a text message, a Facebook

125

message, a WhatsApp message – whichever the other person prefers to use. In the message, ask to meet up for coffee (or whatever) to discuss how to provide value to each other. The structure of your message should be something like:

"Hello

It was great to meet you last night! I enjoyed what you had to say about [topic] – it helped me [how it helped you].

I think we can provide a lot of value to each other. When are you free for coffee?

Thanks

[Name]"

NB: I like to call people as it's far easier to make definite plans and gauge their actual interest in your offer. In addition, email gets lost or misconstrued, whereas a telephone conversation quickly allows you to communicate your position effectively as you can be more emotive over the phone.

Set up a regular contact schedule

IF THEY WOULD LIKE TO MEET YOU, GREAT! You've already succeeded. However, this *rarely* happens. What you need to do is create a database of your contacts. In the database, list all their contact information and, most importantly, when you contacted them, what you spoke about, and when you'll contact them again.

Make sure you ask the other person for the best time to contact them again. Their answer will give you a good indication of what to do next. For example, if you're a marketer, they may tell you that they're launching a new product next year and will need your services a few months before the launch.

On this point, *always* make sure that you know what it is that you want to achieve from the conversation. Have secondary goals should your priority outcome not be viable. For example, recently I spoke to someone in my network about helping them set up a training course. My priority outcome is to go into business with them; my next priority is to understand their goals for the training course and the skillsets that I bring to create their training course; my final goal is to continue a win-win relationship where they can provide value using their skills and I can help them with my skillset.

Similarly, once you've set up a meeting or scheduled a phone call, make sure that you prep the other person about what you want to discuss. Treat the meeting like you would any other business meeting; send them an agenda with a summary of what you spoke about last time, the reason that you're meeting, and the topics that you'd like to discuss. You will save so much time when you set agendas!

To build a good connection with someone, create a regular contact schedule. When you make sure that *you* are in the forefront of their minds you save them the drudgery of having to look for someone with your skill set.

Tailor your approach

IF YOU'RE SERIOUS ABOUT DOING BUSINESS with someone, make it easy for them to talk to you. Use *their* preferred platforms, speak to them via their ideal medium, and understand their communication style.

By platform I mean whether they prefer to use webmail, LinkedIn, Facebook, or WhatsApp, etc.

By medium we're talking text messages, email, instant messaging, letters, phone calls, and carrier pigeons (if they really want).

By communication style we're looking at: how direct you can be, changing the content based on their personality, and figuring out how they best absorb information.

When communicating with people the most powerful attribute you can have is *adaptability*. For example, when someone is trying to sell a product, they will have different responses. Some will want to know how the product makes them feel whereas others may just want to know what the product does and how it will help them or their business, and how much it costs, that's *it*.

In business (and life), it helps to be intuitive about the other person's wants. Luckily, you can always *ask* them what they think. A good comment would be "Thank you for your time. What's your preferred medium for communication? What kind of information do you find useful, and what kind of information do you find useless?"

Be sure to look after this information. This information will make it easier to share the details of this client with other colleagues in your team and so make your service to the client more professional. Similarly, note any interesting things about this person: things like hobbies, kids, travel plans they've made, favourite food – basically anything that will help you tailor your solution to what they need. Another benefit of saving this information is that it shows the other person they are not just another prospect you're looking to mine for resources.

LinkedIn 101: Leveraging your network

AS PREVIOUSLY MENTIONED, LinkedIn is a valuable resource that is often overlooked by people. Its biggest advantage is that you can passively communicate information to people without contacting everybody individually, the same way Facebook has a News Feed.

Remember to use the right social medium for the right business and demographics. Social media sites such as LinkedIn are great for corporate engagements but not so good for consumers. In addition, LinkedIn has some *great* features to help increase your personal branding and network online.

In this section, you will learn about strategies to help you remain in people's thoughts and provide value to your network. The psychology that makes this work is the idea that 1) people assume that social media provides an accurate slice of real life, and 2) they also want to provide high value to others.

Unlike Facebook, people often feel more justified

in browsing LinkedIn. When you provide high quality content that helps people, they will want to know more about what you and how you can help them.

MESSAGING

Messaging people on LinkedIn is an excellent way of contacting people whose email address you *don't have*. The messaging function on LinkedIn is perfunctory and, unless you're in sales, people don't spend that much time checking through their LinkedIn messages.

To use myself as an example, I go on LinkedIn about once a week. I'll be on there more if I'm looking to hire someone, have had a heavy month of networking, or if someone has sent me a LinkedIn message (I get alerts to my email).

There are two ways to use LinkedIn messaging. The first is that, because it's less frequently seen than an email, the person is far more likely to see it and respond to it. The second is that they may not use LinkedIn that much so your message may go unseen for a while.

Use your intuition to gauge how receptive this person is to using LinkedIn as a messaging platform; ask yourself:

- How quickly do they respond?

- How warm were they with their response?

- Do they use the messaging service more like email or more like WhatsApp?

- When you message someone on LinkedIn (or on any platform) you need to have one of the following two objectives in mind:

  o Setting up a meeting

  o Building rapport

Some companies use LinkedIn to obtain email addresses and phone numbers. After that, they call or email people when they want to contact them as it's a more effective way of communicating.

SHARE YOUR VISION/BUSINESS DIRECTION

If you hope to engage with your LinkedIn contacts at *any* point in the future, it's important to keep them abreast of the current news in your business life and organization. We stress business life – so please no news about your domestic issues (unless that is your business).

One feature in LinkedIn that allows you to keep everyone abreast of your current situation is its blog feature. The blog feature enables you to post articles that you've enjoyed or written. Your blog posts will also show people you're connected with what your passions are and how you do business.

Your goal here - as it should be with most aspects of your business - is to help people, by providing them with helpful information that they may not have had before. However, you can also use this technique to share with people the various changes you've made to your business.

For example, if you've recently overhauled your workflow processes, post (or better yet, write) an article about some ways that people can analyse their own processes and improve them. With the post include the comment: "We've spent the last month optimising our business processes; here's what we've learned."

The post shows people that your business is better than it was previously, *and* that you love helping people succeed themselves.

An additional bonus of this post is that you know people who comment are interested in the ideas contained within the post, and may be receptive to doing business with you.

YOUR PROFILE

If you regularly post useful articles on LinkedIn, more people will be attracted to view your profile; this is why you need to make your profile as useful as possible.

Use your profile to answer the questions you should be asking people at networking events and each month update your profile to reflect current projects and the things you'd like help with.

Also, because it's your profile, people won't be shocked when you put your best foot forward. Continually update it to reflect the achievements that you're proud of.

Your profile is also a great place to summarise what drives you, and how you like to conduct business. Think of your profile as a filter for people who you want to work with. Your LinkedIn design should create a list of services you're looking for and a list of qualities that you like. Ask people who think they have those qualities to send you a message.

Everyone is always looking for talented people, and you're no different. At any one time, there are thousands of great people who are looking to change roles, work on new projects, or who just want a fresh start.

Chapter 5 Key take-aways

FOLLOW-UP AND CONSISTENCY IS KEY

IF YOU KEEP AT SOMETHING LONG ENOUGH, you're guaranteed to see results. Be consistent. Make sure that you incorporate building relationships into your daily schedule, and eventually your network will be at a size where you will continually be offered opportunities.

The takeaways from this are:

Follow up fast: If you had a great conversation with someone, invite them for coffee ASAP. You've already built some fantastic momentum, don't waste it!

Set up a schedule: Contacts turn into relationships through continual effort; if a meeting can't be created, ask them when they'd like to have a sit down with you.

LinkedIn is your best friend: LinkedIn is a mass

communication tool that you can use to demonstrate who you are and what your business can do.

Post stuff: Share/write/make things that will help people and put them on LinkedIn. Even if someone isn't interested in it, it builds your reputation.

Pimp your profile: Think of your profile as your first impression, put as much care into it as you would a dating profile.

Chapter 5 Exercises

LINKEDIN EXERCISE

If you do not have a LinkedIn account, spend a few hours creating one. If you're stuck for ideas here are ours. Use them as templates and insert your own information:

Nate Chai's – https://www.linkedin.com/in/nate-chai-9411b956/

Ben Chai's
https://www.linkedin.com/in/chaiben/

LINKEDIN EXERCISE 2

Get as many testimonials from colleagues, bosses or people you've done business with. These testimonials should have some insight to your character. A good testimonial includes:

- The result that you created

- The work that you put in

- Why they would work with you again

LINKEDIN EXERCISE 3

Write three 500-word articles about some aspect of your business you are passionate about and how people can improve their businesses in those aspects.

Publish these articles once a week, and see how much more attention your profile gets.

CHAPTER 6:
How to Make Networking a Fun Habit

A HUGE BLOCKAGE FOR PEOPLE when it comes to networking, is the idea that it's always in a stuffy hotel somewhere. Everyone who's there is in a suit or business attire and the conversation is *dry*.

Treat networking and business events as a play-date for adults. Even when you are at a networking event and you meet someone who has the skill set and knowledge that will help you with a project, you may not proceed with anything other than a conversation. Your reason?

You don't *like* them.

And that's not to say that there's anything wrong with them, you just don't feel like you want to work with them. Call it "chemistry", call it "personality types", call it an "x-factor", if the other person doesn't have it, you're not going further with that relationship.

If you're going to do business with someone you need to think "Would you be happy doing business with this person in the future?" If the answer is "No" then any long-term venture you try will end up being a huge waste of time.

A quirk of the human condition is that our emotions guide our decision making far more than logic, and to network effectively you need to find people that you can connect with on both an emotional and logical level.

With that in mind, where do you think you'll find the highest number of people who you can connect with both logically and emotionally? Answer this question first: *Where* do we socially *express* ourselves? Or more specifically: *Where* do *I* socially express myself?

In this chapter, you will learn some great techniques for you to answer that question for yourself. You will also discover the best places for you to network, where you feel most comfortable, and the places most likely to attract *your* type of people. Let's look at places outside of a business event such as a class or social event where you may be able to network more effectively.

Learn stuff everywhere

THE CLASSROOM IS A GREAT PLACE TO NETWORK because you never know *who* is going to be attending the class. You can meet a wide variety of individuals and get the chance to see how they operate. Over time you'll understand their motives, their diligence, and their goals. The bonus of networking in a classroom is that you know you all have an interest in bettering yourself in that subject.

In many ways, the classroom is the same as a work environment. You're all there to achieve a goal, having to problem solve situations that you're unfamiliar with, and work with people who you may not normally spend time with. As a result, you can see which people quickly grasp concepts, which diligently do their homework each week, and how they interact when they're doing group tasks.

For my fellow introverts out there, starting a conversation during/after a class is much simpler than approaching someone at a formally organised networking event. The two of you already have something in common, and to break the ice you can discuss the topics raised in the class.

Another great benefit about the classroom is the sheer variety of people you meet. Typically, when you attended professional networking events, you'll see the same sorts of people – people who come from very similar walks of life, and who have the same values and beliefs. This is fantastic if you're looking for a *specific* type of person.

However, when you attend a class to learn a subject you more than likely will spend ten or more hours with the people in your class. For example, I once took a course titled "Emotional Intelligence in the Workplace." In the class, I met people from all over the world, each with different professions, and different perspectives on life.

By using the classroom as a tool for self-improvement *and* networking you dramatically increase the return on your investment. And now you have an even better excuse to take that scuba-diving course you've always wanted to do!

Do something you enjoy socially

WHEN I WAS YOUNGER my Dad *made* me take dancing lessons, and I hated him for it. However, on reflection, I realised that he was teaching me that "networking" doesn't necessarily mean "people in suits milling around a stuffy room".

From dancing, I've met so many people who have become friends, business partners, mentors, mentees, and even the odd girlfriend. Through dance classes, dancing events, and dancing nights, I've met a staggering array of people who I can help, and who want to help me.

What makes attending social events so great for networking is that you don't need to think about your "elevator pitch" or your "networking strategy". All you need to do is go, have a good time, and talk to people. Inevitably they'll ask what you do, and you'll (assuming you've practiced doing the exercises in Chapters 1 to 3) have an engaging answer.

Dance is a great way to connect with people as it is

inherently social. You need to have physical contact with someone, talk to them, and communicate. However, any activity that forces you to be around people with similar hobbies to you will yield the same results. You can meet great people at comic book clubs, board game nights, pub quizzes, and, even Star Trek conventions.

If you're stuck for ideas about what to do, try using a social networking service like MeetUp.com and browse for groups in your area. A common complaint from people who live in small villages is that there are not enough local events. Gemma, the copy editor for this book offered this tip:

"I live in the countryside and there can be quite a lot going on (although not to the scale of cities). Local websites (e.g. town/village websites, local council websites, etc) and local libraries can be a good place to find out what is going on (especially for classes and social events)."

If there are absolutely no events in your area, then use online forums that discuss subjects in your area or your target client's area.

Somewhere relaxing

ONE THING MANY *DISLIKE* ABOUT NETWORKING EVENTS is how "on" people are. It's like they've activated "networking mode" and aren't being authentic. When you meet people, the ultimate goal is for you to present who you are honestly and without pretence. This skill will come with practice, but in the meantime, try networking in relaxing environments.

At networking events, it feels like many attendees are in a rush; they only have two hours to meet someone who specifically has the skillset and knowledge required. In a more relaxed setting you skip the elevator pitch, and the jargon, and focus more on having a decent conversation.

These kinds of places are ones that are inherently social but where sociability isn't the place's primary purpose. Places that serve food and drink are great for this vibe. Places such as coffee shops, restaurants, and markets – believe or now I've met some great places in restaurants who have invested in our businesses or who have just become great friends. You also need to look for places where people have enough time for a five- to ten-minute conversation. In general coffee shops are best, due to there being less distractions and less interruptions with questions about food and drink.

Now you might be thinking "What if they can't help me with my business?" The chances are that they can't, but time is never wasted when spent on making a new friend. Many people we have done business with has been as an indirect recommendation of our new friend.

One example shared from a friend was when he was in an Indian restaurant. He spotted a gentleman eating alone and struck up a conversation with him. The conversation naturally flowed to their professions. When he told the gentleman that he currently renovates property, his jaw *dropped*. The gentleman then shared that he was the owner of a block of flats in the town next to his and he was looking to sell them quickly. What a lovely business opportunity.

This doesn't happen every time, but you'll be surprised at how "lucky" you get once you start saying "hello" to strangers.

The best places to network

BUSINESS EVENTS ARE A GREAT EXPERIENCE but frankly, they are not the only place to find great business contacts. You've already seen examples of dance events, meeting strangers in restaurants and parties.

"Networking" is about the ability to connect and make friends. Networking events are great places to find like-minded people but are *not* the be all and end all of meeting people. To prove the point, I have already done business with several people in my local town. When friends come and visit they are surprised by how many local townspeople know me by name and want to stop and have a conversation.

By spending time doing things that you want to do, and turning them into social occasions you'll find a smorgasbord of friends, business partners, and opportunities.

The classroom: Here you can see how people work doing something that they're passionate about.

A social club: A great informal way to meet people with whom you share an interest. You never know who you'll meet.

Somewhere relaxing: Now you can network without all the *network*-iness of formally arranged events.

Getting into the habit

IN THIS SECTION, YOU WILL LEARN TECHNIQUES that will help improve your networking habits and make it a regular part of your life.

The challenge faced by creating new habits is that they take on average 21 days to form. The challenge with networking is that it's tough to find, and do, 21 days of solid networking. If you have ever been to a week of solid networking you will appreciate how *exhausting* it is.

As previously mentioned, if you have the time, attend one networking event a week. Although, realistically, you'll probably only have time to attend one or two a month. The key *isn't* how many events you attend a month, but your regularity and consistency. Set yourself the goal of "networking" every other week; similarly, try to attend at least one class a week and some sort of communal hobby-based activity once a week.

Here are several tried and tested techniques experienced networkers have used to build awesome networks.

TECHNIQUE 1: THE "HELLO" EFFECT

The "hello" technique is the most effective way to begin a conversation. On a personal note, I used to be ultra-nervous about initially going up to people and *talking* to them. I logic-ed that because I'd had conversations with people before I wasn't scared of that aspect. The part that I was afraid of was *starting* a conversation with someone.

So, I began starting as many conversations as I could. This translated to greeting people in the street who were walking toward me (initially terrifying). Anyone who passed me, I'd offer a "Hello" or a "Good morning/afternoon". I'd set myself goals to greet at least one person when I was out walking; then, after a week of that, I'd go for five.

Now it's just a natural part of my life. After two weeks of trying this exercise, you'll see that most people are friendly and are accepting of a friendly greeting. The reason why greeting people who are walking past you is so fantastic for starting out is because there's no commitment to have a conversation. You just say "Hello", and continue walking along.

TECHNIQUE 2: THE LONG-LOST FRIEND APPROACH

One technique that is super beneficial when you approach someone is to imagine that they're a friend who you haven't seen in a while. I discovered this well-used technique by accident when I was in a coffee shop. At the time, I saw someone I thought I knew and went over to chat to them, as I approached I had a smile on my face and gave them a warm "Hey!"

It wasn't them!

Despite my embarrassment, the reaction from this person was unlike any I'd received from a stranger before. It was almost like *she* thought I was a friend from her past that she'd misplaced in her memory.

Here's how you can use this technique. Think about how *you* would approach someone who you haven't seen in a few years. Now whenever you see someone who you'd like to talk to, use the same energy, body language, and tonality when you go over and say hello.

TECHNIQUE 3: THE COFFEE INVITE

One of my biggest challenges in networking was my inability to follow up encounters with potential business partners with a meeting. The *only* reason for this was simple. I *wasn't* asking them!

End encounters that you have with "When are you free for coffee?" Again, I know that this can be scary, so set yourself goals similar to the "saying hello" exercise. Ironically, this exercise is *far* easier when you say it to a lot of people.

The reason it's easier to ask a *lot* of people, is because you'll find out how many people would *love* to go have coffee with you. Once you get comfortable, saying it at the end of conversations, you'll have to *stop* yourself from saying it so you don't spend the rest of your life drinking coffee with other people!

As you become more experienced, the patterns of

people who *genuinely* want to spend time with you will become more obvious.

TECHNIQUE 4: THE DETAIL SWAP

Our fourth and final technique for building great networks is to end every encounter by getting contact details (Facebook, phone number, or business card). Do this immediately even if it is simply to add the person's social media details on the spot. Whether it be their Facebook, Twitter, Instagram or other details provided it is a social media account that they use often.

Social media is great at creating authentic conversations because you are indirectly sharing things about your passions and life with others. After a while, you can quickly see which people you can add value to directly and which ones you can add value indirectly.

Many have used their Facebook accounts to connect with so many people today, some of which they have done business with, others have become great friends and even life partners.

Chapter 6 Key take-Aways

YOUR FUN NETWORKING HABITS

I HOPE YOU'VE FOUND THIS CHAPTER ON HABITS INSPIRING. It is easy to become a network expert and to be known as an expert in this area because so many are bad it. However, although becoming a network expert is easy, it does take time. Take time to learn the habits outlined in this chapter. Make everyday a fun learning experience in networking.

Once you become an expert, we hope you will contact us and share some of your adventures and in return we will give you some advanced techniques that will totally take your networking to a different level. Remember the goal of becoming a social magnet so constantly add value and learn to connect rather than just network.

Here is a reminder on how to make networking more enjoyable.

Nothing is personal: Don't get offended if someone is rude to you. We don't know what has happened to them in their personal life or their own goals for attending an event.

Learn stuff everywhere: Use every situation as an opportunity to network. Say "Hello" to strangers, shop owners and be ready to answer the questions "How are you and what do you do?"

Network socially: Networking doesn't just happen in business situations. Join a club or take a class and endeavour to network with others in the group.

Follow-up all contacts: Invite them for a drink or create an online conversation with them using some of the popular social media sites such as Facebook.

Get the network habit: Network, network, network. Network until you can get a 100 per cent success rate in making people smile and creating a good general energy.

Chapter 6 Exercises

JOIN A GROUP

In Chapters 1 and 2, you created a list of the areas you were knowledgeable or skilled in. In this exercise, find as many classes or clubs in your area that cater to your particular interest.

Sign up for one that seems most appropriate and fun to you. When you arrive decide if it is a class/club you would like to attend regularly. If not continue searching.

NETWORK EVENT

Have you got an interest in dance, property investing, football, languages or network marketing? Many of these and others have regular monthly meetups.

Commit to attend one for at least six months. Even

if you decide it is not for you, ensure you network and make friends.

CREATE A FACEBOOK ACCOUNT

Create an account on Facebook or whatever other social media sites your peer groups are involved with. You do not need to make a post; however, your account will enable you to take part in online conversations with people you meet at events. In today's society, being in social media is essential if you are interested in growing your social and business network.

CHAPTER 7:
Networking on Social Media

UNDERSTANDING HOW TO NETWORK EFFECTIVELY using social media is a must. We live in an integrated world where our online virtual and physical presence impact on one another. Any and all good work you have done at a networking event can be totally obliterated by a bad social media post.

In previous chapters, we've mentioned LinkedIn and Facebook as key components of networking. It is essential that you understand the impact your social media has on others and how it portrays you to the world. If every post you make is of food, you will be known as a foodie, if all you have are posts of cats, then you will be labelled a cat-lover.

Networking on social media has helped us raise finance for large projects, find great people to help us complete projects and to add value to the wider community around. By added-value, I mean, creating great photographs from events that everyone can share, connecting people we met from one event to people from other events.

Here we will focus on the essentials of online

conversation for LinkedIn, Facebook, Twitter and YouTube. These essentials can be applied to any social media.

LinkedIn conversations

WE HAVE ALREADY SHARED A LOT IN OUR PREVIOUS chapter on LinkedIn. LinkedIn is one of the best social media sites for engaging in a business. The LinkedIn user's profile quickly tells you all about them and whether they are the best person to have a business discussion with. Several of my CEO friends have used LinkedIn to recruit people and attract several high net worth orders. As a quick recap:

- Get your profile set-up. Ensure the profile is consistent with what you to share with people at events.

- Try to write the answers to the profile questions as if you were having a conversation at an event. These answers should be brief but should leave conversational hooks should someone wish to engage in deeper discussion.

- Obtain as many testimonials as you can.

In the basic (free) LinkedIn site you are provided with several opportunities to converse with people.

Use the LinkedIn (or Google) search facility to find people you may wish to employ or work for. Within LinkedIn create a chat session with the person. If they are online and willing, they will respond quickly in the chat box. If not, they will have an email of your request to chat with them.

Use the LinkedIn articles comments section to leave comments about the articles. In general, try to build on the premise of the article or praise the author. Avoid saying anything that may be construed as negative as forum "fights and flame wars" are seen by everyone beyond your friend group and will be on record for as long as the article is onsite.

If you have met someone at a network event and you are now both linked, send that person a friendly message. Check out their profile and if appropriate set-up a coffee meetup. Use your LinkedIn connection to send them articles relevant to their interests and job.

Facebook

FACEBOOK IS ANOTHER GREAT WAY TO NETWORK and engage with others. As mentioned earlier Facebook has enabled us to raise finance for property and business projects, make new friends and even helped to connect friends who have now become life partners.

Conversely, we have also seen many people fall out or be devalued because of their Facebook posts. To help you avoid these traps, let's recap the conversational rules. Break these at your own risk.

FACEBOOK POSTS TO AVOID

The first and most important social rule is the same as in the network events you attend. Just as in the face to face network events avoid commenting and engaging in politics, religion and sex.

Now I have friends who comment about these subjects all the time, however they are special in that they are not interested in having friends outside of their belief system. As a result of their sometimes rude and abusive posts, these friends are constantly defriending others or being so abusive to their people's belief systems that they themselves are defriended.

If you like someone as a person, but you don't like what someone is posting you can mute their posts but still keep them as a friend. If you don't like them as a person, then it is best to defriend them.

The second Facebook mistake people make is to copy and share chain posts. These are the posts that have **copy/share** at the end. For example, one common chain post is "Bill Gate's has promised to donate $1 for every person that shares this post!" Incredible! 99 percent of these posts have probably been created to guilt or motivate people into sharing them and most are bogus anyway. Before sharing any of these posts, google their authenticity or better don't ever post them.

The third Facebook mistake is to make constant sales and marketing posts. Remember if your Facebook wall looks like a constant sales pitch, people will believe that you are exactly the same in real life. Facebook has a facility that allows you to create your own adverts so use that facility rather than impact on the authenticity of your character.

FACEBOOK POSTS TO ENGAGE IN

Other than politics, sex and religion, post whatever you like. Share the pictures of your new born, your cat, a fantastic meal, your holiday. These are all great. However, don't just post about these. For example, one person we coached is one of the most awesome gas engineers.

Her Facebook posts consisted predominantly of all the friendly things we shared about, but her business was suffering. We suggested that she continue posting all her usual posts but also added that she post at least one success or business lesson that she had experienced that week.

Not immediately, but over a few months she got two new orders from large companies. Remember that what you post is how people will perceive you. Even if your Facebook is a private friends and family only Facebook, post at least one success/failure story a week. In the failure story, put the lesson learned.

How to create a Facebook strategy

EVERY YEAR I CREATE A FACEBOOK STRATEGY. Ensure you make at least one post every week. At time of writing, I have Mindset Monday, Property Tuesday, Celebrity Wednesday. In a previous year, I had Feel the Fear Wednesday, Tricky Thursday and Parenting Friday.

On each of those days I would post something relevant to that day. For example, on Mindset Monday, I would make at least one post about useful mindset or thoughts I had from the previous week.

On Property Tuesday, I would post pictures of the latest property I'd viewed, or make a post about some lessons I'd learned with regard to property investment.

On Celebrity Wednesday, I would post a picture of me and a well-known or an industry celebrity I'd met and some of the conversation I had with them.

The impact of making these posts every week caused my Facebook connections to label me as a person who knows a lot of celebrities and is successful in property. Note these posts were in addition to my normal family and out and about pictures.

CONVERSATIONS IN FACEBOOK

Networking is about creating connections and participating in conversations, so learn to comment on other people's posts. Where-ever possible keep your comments as positive as you can. Keep your initial comments light until you get to know the other person better.

Try to add value in subjects you are knowledgeable about. For example, if you see a post about a Facebook's friend's child suffering from eczema and you've suffered from eczema, share your own perspective. If the conversation seems like it is getting quite involved, you may offer to have a private message (pm) with your Facebook friend. If appropriate, in the personal message, you may wish to share your phone number and set up a time for a face to face meet-up.

FACEBOOK FLAMING

Occasionally, for absolutely no reason apparent to you, your Facebook friend may become quite aggravated. If possible, have the conversation in the personal message. Where-ever possible avoid arguments on forums and walls. Although it may be great entertainment for other Facebook participants, it is unlikely to do you much good. If the other person is insistent on arguing with you or calling you names – disengage. Senseless arguments and point scoring wastes your valuable time and will not benefit anyone, and certainly not your reputation.

If the person persists in any kind of name-calling, delete the posts they found offensive and block them. Don't give any warning.

Other Social Media Sites

BUILDING YOUR FACEBOOK AND LINKEDIN FRIENDS is relatively straightforward compared to other social media outlets. To build up a YouTube, Twitter, and Instagram account following will depend on the types of value posts you make, the hashtags and keywords you use.

As the social media sites grow, they will add more facilities for you to engage. For example, many sites now have a live video feed which uses your phone to create on-the-spot videos. This live video feed is a great way to share how you are and a little about your business successes. Try and set aside a specific time every week to share a bit of news in the video feed.

Should you have the time and dedication to grow a large following then you can have many conversations through the comment section and message other users directly. The same rules will apply as per conversations in Facebook and LinkedIn however you may have to deal with two extra conversational challenges promoters and haters. Haters are a bi-product of how famous you become.

The conversational challenges from promoters are that promoters will create adverts that appear all over your personal spaces. Haters will write text messages and create videos about you. Simply by becoming successful is a good enough reason for them to have a dislike for you.

- You have several strategies to deal with both promoters and haters.

- If the sites have the ability to block them. Block them.

- Delete the promoter's posts and hater's comments and block them.

The site may have ability setting to allow you to remain connected with a promoter but prevent the promoter from posting on your profile. Check if the site has the setting, only if the promoter becomes a problem and you still do not wish to block them.

Chapter 7 Key take-aways

INTEGRATE SOCIAL MEDIA WITH SOCIAL LIFE

To SOCIALISE IN AN INTEGRATED WORLD, it is essential that you participate in social media and you know how to conduct yourself. Remember all the rules of face to face conversation apply but certain aspects may become magnified.

Participate in online conversations: At worst send a happy birthday or click on like of a post. This "like" lets your social media friend know you are out there and reading their posts.

Always try to add value: Build on conversations in some way. Until you know your social media friend better try to keep your comments light. If the situation demands, ask for a personal message and from the personal message invite your social media friend for a meeting.

Make special days: Have days about things that you're passionate about (e.g. "Mate Mondays" where you promote your mate) and set times for a particular time of post and/or live video.

Be Selective: People are more likely to be rude online, so be ready to block without discussion.

Avoid copying and sharing chain messages: The majority are either scams or prey on making the reader guilty and will impact people's perspectives of your authenticity.

Never post anything about blocking or clearing out your friends: If you are going to do it, just do it otherwise people will feel you are an attention seeker with no real value to offer anyone.

Social media can be addictive Set yourself a time limit and never replace face to face events with social media networking.

In social media, start with quantity: As you attract more and more social media friends start replacing people you never converse with. Choose higher quality social media friends that you have more in common with or want to follow because of their inspirational posts.

Chapter 7 Exercises

FACEBOOK PROFILE CREATION EXERCISE

If you have not already done so, create a Facebook page and ask all your close friends to be your Facebook friend.

Write down a time each week that you will post about a business success. Be sure to make the post non-salesy.

Write down a time each week that you will use Facebook Live to create a short one to two-minute video on your thoughts for the week.

GROUP JOIN EXERCISE

Join three Facebook forums or groups that cater for your interests. Follow the administrator rules, so if they ask you to introduce yourself do so.

Once you have successfully been admitted to the group. Make a comment on three separate posts. Create a schedule to do this once every week.

CHAPTER 8:
The Networking Golden Rule

I'M SO GLAD YOU'VE MADE IT TO THE FINAL CHAPTER. Hopefully you've realised from the information, techniques, and exercises shared in this book that "networking" isn't as scary as it originally appeared to be, nor does it have to be boring and formulaic.

It can take you from months to years to get good at networking and ultimately becoming a social magnet. Two important attitudes will help with how fast your social magnetism is magnified. The first attitude is to attend as many networking events as possible preferably a minimum of two a week.

The second attitude is to be an objective learner. As an objective learner, at the end of every event, list every conversation that went well and why it went well. Then list all the things that didn't seem to go well and think about how you can improve the next time. By being objective, you remove your emotions from the situation which will help prevent your ego and negative thoughts get you down.

There is an easy fix to solving all your networking woes. It is, perhaps, surprising how many people already know the golden rule of networking, and apply it to many aspects of their life but *not* to "networking".

The golden rule of networking (as with living a just life) is...

Do unto others as you would have them do unto you.

Do you want people to constantly make sales pitches to you?

WHEN I WAS A LOWLY JOURNALISTIC INTERN one task was to meet as many people possible at trade events and conventions. Meeting these people would ensure my publication would have access to the best news available.

I spoke to hundreds of product reps, PR people, and business development professionals. Without even finding out a little about me, they would launch into their well-rehearsed, two-minute-long, jargon-filled, product pitch. This wasted our time, because networking isn't about selling.

The clue is in the title "networking"; it's about building a network of people who *you* can benefit and who can benefit *you*.

Unless someone is in the market for something, it's useless trying to sell them something. It's so annoying when someone pitches a product to you that you have no interest in buying. The relationship is lopsided.

When you have a product to sell, remember that the purpose of a networking event is to *build relationships and create deep connections*.

Time wasting

WOULD YOU PREFER SOMEONE WHO POLITELY LISTENS to you or someone who enables you to use your time effectively? A common complaint from people at business events, is that they often find themselves "wasting time" talking to someone who doesn't align with their goals. Being stuck in a conversation is one of the hardest things to get out of, due to all the faux pas that can make you seem rude.

However, everyone at the event has a goal. Everyone has decided to be at that place, at that time, for a reason. As you evolve your mindset from "I want this person to like me" to "I want to help this person as much as possible," you will often walk away from an unhelpful conversation OR introduce them to someone you think could help them. You are actually being rude when you *waste* someone's valuable networking time; especially when you politely listen to them but have no intention of engaging with them further.

Imagine you've been having a great chat with someone, they seem engaged and interested, *but* after talking to them for 20 minutes they turn around and say, "I don't know if we can help each other." You'd feel cheated, and wish that they'd said something earlier.

Don't be afraid of disengaging from a conversation if you feel that neither of you can benefit each other. There is an art to disengaging that leaves all parties satisfied (See Chapter 4). With that said, take the burden of possible perceived "rudeness" and plainly state "I have a goal to meet five people in this industry by the end of tonight. Do you mind if I see if I can find those people?"

Add value where-ever possible

THERE ARE SEVERAL THINGS YOU CAN TAKE where you won't bring immediate benefits but will vastly improve your ability to connect and have fun. Find ways to increase everyone's enjoyment/effectiveness at the event; here are a few great techniques:

Talk with people who are alone: Imagine that you were standing alone at a networking event, one of the best confidence-boosting things someone could do for you is to simply come and make them feel welcome.

Get people drinks: If you notice someone doesn't have a drink/has finished their drink, offer to get them and the group more refreshments. This gives you time to think about what they've said *and* increases your rapport. Don't over-do it, as you will seem too needy and will annoy people when you constantly interrupt their conversation by constantly asking them if they would like you to refill their cups.

Do other people's networking for them: Even if you can't help someone with your skill set, there is someone in the room who can. Help others connect with people you've already met who have similar attitudes and goals.

Take selfies and group photographs: if the event allows, people love having photographs taken especially when you ask for a selfie with them. Be sure you post the picture in social media with a description of what you enjoyed most about talking with your new acquaintance.

NB: At some events such as ones we attend in cyber security, people don't like their photographs taken so be sensitive to the event.

By doing small favours for others you'll attract the people who notice these little details, and who will genuinely want to help you. They may not be able to help you *now*, but the future is a strange place and it's amazing who you end up meeting later in your life.

Your mindset is the key

BY TREATING OTHERS HOW YOU EXPECT TO BE TREATED you'll find people who are most in tune with what you're looking to accomplish. You'll also stand out from the Me-Me-Me crowd that still permeates through a lot of the networking scene. Have the following mantras in mind whenever you go out to meet people:

- I will help people whenever I can

- I will learn from my mistakes

- I will speak to people the way I want to be spoken to

- I will not take rejection personally

- I will always thank people who have inspired or helped me

CHAPTER 9:
Your Network = Your Net Worth

A STRONG VIBRANT NETWORK IS WORTH MORE than all the money in the bank. Whenever you are in any kind of difficulty your network will be there to actively support and work with you through your challenges.

Over my years on this planet, I have been fortunate to build a great network that can and has supported me in a variety of crises and helped me to develop and grow businesses. Should I become homeless or trapped somewhere on this planet, there are people who will instantly come to my aid at no extra cost.

Let me share a personal example. A while back, a betrayal occurred in which I was left in a lot of debt. My network rallied round to support me with no interest loans and all kinds of emotional support. Over the years several people have tried to spread all types of negative stuff about me on social media, my network has always been there and in fact the gossipers/haters were banned from events for spreading their malicious gossip.

If you build your network correctly, you will never

be in need. Your network will help you find life partners, new opportunities, jobs, customers and help you in ways you could never imagine. I have been sold properties by my network which have been substantially below market price all because they loved me and wanted to bless me in some way.

The number one reason for that is the value that I've given them. Value comes in all types of forms. We've shared the types of value you can give at hosted events but you can give all types of value to others outside the event.

I live in a small suburb just outside London. The majority of shop owners in the suburb know me. If I have left my money at home, they have either given me goods for free or trusted that I would return with the money to pay for their goods. Many of the food outlets are constantly giving me extra food or inviting me to come ahead of queues.

Network everywhere and with everyone. Where ever possible stay in contact with everyone including former colleagues and business partners (assuming no betrayals have been involved). The best people to network with and keep in your life are people, who no matter what their social level, have a great mindset and believe in and will support you in your failures and your successes.

To build this network you have to make the same commitment to them. They will only see that commitment in your actions.

Good luck in all you do and please do send us a message if anything we have shared in this book has helped you moved forward in any part of your life.

About the Author

Ben Chai is considered by many to be the hidden jewel in the international speaking and coaching world.

Ben is considered a jewel because he has lived his talk. Every single nugget of business and mindset strategy, Ben shares with you, Ben has actioned to grow a variety of seven-figure businesses in diverse fields including property, software, media, authoring, security, education, and hospitality.

Much of his success in both his businesses and his personal life has been due to his ability to attract accomplished people, great investors and authentic business people into his life.

His insights and his generosity to share from the stage, on a 1-1 basis, and from his broadcasts have helped hundreds of thousands of people in over 70 countries reach new levels of greatness in their lives.

Today Ben runs several property and media businesses and is an executive advisor and equity holder in others. When he is not in business mode, you can find him watching superhero films, salsa dancing or educating himself further in other subjects.

Websites and Media:

www.FiveYearsToFinancialFreedom.com

https://www.facebook.com/benchaipublic

https://www.facebook.com/BenInsightChai/

Acknowledgments

This book is a mixture of old and new. Many examples are from Nate's life as well as my own. Due to my many engagements, without Nate, the release of this book would not have been possible. Much of my own personal development in networking and socialization has been through reading Dale Carnegie's "How to Win Friends and Influence People" together with the works of Wayne Dyer and Earl Nightingale.

Other people who taught me a lot about socialization was my university friend Thana Shanmugam who has a massive hospitality gift, my first sales manager, Alan Mackelworth who runs one of the largest networking groups, Johnny Cassell, a dating coach who later became a good friend, my daughter Jessica who helped me learn how to hug people, my ex-wife Rachel Chai who always has something positive to say about someone.

I'd also like to thank Marian Gazdik, the European Director of StartUp Grind, for being an incredible dancer and showing me how life-changing being a great networker can be.

Last but not least, I'd also like to acknowledge you, the reader and the many people at the events who gave me feedback about what they did/didn't like about me when they first met me.

Made in the USA
Las Vegas, NV
04 February 2021

17223089R00115